Life Journeys: Love and Grief

Also by Satendra Nandan
Ashes and Waves
Girmit: Epic Lives in Small Lines
Gandhianjali
1987 – Six Nights in May
Across the Seven Seas
Nadi: Memories of a River
Seashells on the Seashore:
A Pair of Black Shoes and Other Stories
Beyond Paradise: Rights of Passage
The Loneliness of Islands
Requiem for a Rainbow:
A Fijian Indian Story
Lines Across Black Waters
The Wounded Sea
Voices in the River
Faces in a Village
Dispatches From Distant Shores
Brief Encounters: Literature & Beyond
Between the Lines
Fiji: Paradise in Pieces
India-Fiji (co-editor)
Australasian Encounters (co-editor)
Resistance and Reconciliation (co-editor)
Crossing Cultures (co-editor)
Silverfish New Writing (editor)
Creative Writing from Fiji (co-editor)
Language and Literature in Multicultural Contexts (editor)

Satendra Nandan

Life Journeys: Love and Grief

For Jyoti, my love

Life Journeys: Love and Grief
ISBN 978 1 76109 404 0
Copyright © text Satendra Nandan 2022
Cover design: Phil Knight
Cover photo: Phil Knight, Sunset over Kennedy Island, Solomon Sea, Solomon Islands, 2017

First published 2022 by
Ginninderra Press
PO Box 3461 Port Adelaide 5015
www.ginninderrapress.com.au

Contents

Acknowledgements	7
Foreword	9
Preface	13
1. Leaving	17
2. Heart's Journeys	57
3. The House That Ivy Built	122
4. Return Flight to Paradise	171
5. A Remembrance	199
Afterword	213
About the Author	215

Acknowledgements

This book was written some time ago to be published in March 2021. Covid-19 intervened, hence the delay while life has been disrupted for most of us.

During this period, I requested my friend Professor Will Christie to write a foreword. I'm delighted he found time to read the manuscript and pen a moving foreword.

Later, Jyoti and I had lunch with Dr Gillian Dooley, former editor of *Transnational Literatures*, from Adelaide. Gillian has had a deep interest in our world and has visited Fiji and India. She agreed to browse through the pages and write an afterword.

My special thanks to Stephen Matthews for publishing this volume – our old Canberra friendship renewed with affectionate gratitude.

The cover has been designed by Philip Knight from Vancouver, Canada. Phil and I were colleagues on the Fiji Constitution Commission to draft Fiji's fourth constitution after four coups. Phil, a poet and photographer, designed this extraordinary cover for my book as he did for *Gandhianjali*, dedicated to my daughter Gitanjali.

To Jyoti this volume is dedicated. Jyoti read the first draft of my book of memories. I wanted our children, grandchildren, to know the journeys their parents-grandparents had made in the last sixty years together.

Foreword

It will become apparent to those who read the obituary for Ian Donaldson with which Satendra Nandan closes his reflections on the gratifications and frustrations of his own rich and clearly rewarding life that the author's history with the Humanities Research Centre (HRC) at the Australian National University dates back more than forty years to the 1970s, when as a student of the new area topic of Commonwealth Literature he came to a country then unknown to him to undertake a PhD on the Australian novelist Patrick White. Born into a once indentured or girmit ('agreement') Indian family in Fiji, and having studied in India and the UK and taught in India and Fiji, Satendra introduced his Australian colleagues to V.S. Naipaul's *A House for Mr Biswas* as he was himself introduced to Australian literature by Bob Brissenden and the poet Alec Hope.

My own period as Director of the HRC dates back a mere seven years to 2015, though I am on familiar terms with its previous directors and share Satendra's great sadness at the recent death of Ian Donaldson, along with the sadness of the many, many scholars throughout the world who knew and loved him. And because of his long association with the HRC, I am also on familiar terms with Satendra and, as such, am honoured to have been asked to write a Foreword to what is a moving and enlightening story about a moving and enlightening man. For if, like A.B. Facey, Satendra can lay claim to 'a fortunate life', it has also been an exemplary life to those of us who aspire to understanding and sympathy across the borders of culture and ethnicity, race and nation.

This is a book about loss, as its author retraces the lives and revisits the deaths of those he has loved most. Satendra ends his reflections with a tribute to Ian and to friendship – the last line of the book is the last line of W.B. Yeats's poem 'The Municipal Gallery Revisited': 'And say my glory was I had such friends'.

Indeed, friendship is at once the glory and the burden of Satendra's narrative, as it is of the book's narrator. What reconciles us to the loss of so many intimates, as he counts down the list of recent funerals and recalls the earlier deaths of those whom he has held dear – what reconciles us to what he deplores in his author's note as 'the fragility of existence and the vulnerability of human life' – is precisely the human relationships that Satendra has established over the course of a full and felt life. First and foremost are his relationships with his beloved Jyoti and their children, Rohan, Gita, and Kavita, his mother-in-law Ivy and other members of his and Jyoti's families, then an endless though recurrent series of no less intense relationships with exceptionally close and supportive friends too many to list here and I hesitate to select for fear of omitting the name of someone important. I say these friendships are both the book's and the author's glory because not only do they make the narrative compelling, they attest to the narrator's generous capacity for love and friendship.

And there is a further propriety in Satendra's choice of Yeats to close the volume, one that probably would never have occurred to him. Perhaps uniquely amongst the canonical poets, Yeats wrote with intellectual and emotional resonance and lyric strength well into old age, and, though the author of many recollections and reflections, Satendra is still able to surprise and move us to revisit our own pasts, and the pastness of the past, in order to rediscover what we thought we already knew.

The great poet of loss, William Wordsworth, talked – sometimes more hopefully than convincingly – of the 'abundant recompense' to be gained for all the 'solitude, or fear, or pain, or grief that necessarily attends upon life. Satendra's reflections on his own life resemble nothing so much as a Wordsworthian elegy in which the consolation he is seeking on his own and on the reader's behalf inheres in the very power and self-evident value of what has been lost:

There is a comfort in the strength of love
'Twill make a thing endurable, which else
Would overset the brain, or break the heart.

> William Christie, Head, Humanities Research Centre,
> Australian National University

Preface

This book came out of recent deaths in my family: Jyoti's older sister Sheilah Philip died in Bangalore in July 2019; soon after, my sister Shiv Kumari Prasad passed away in Auckland. We attended both funerals, having seen them alive a few months before.

One began to experience a sense of an ending at least partially and became aware of both the fragility of existence and the vulnerability of human life: Sheilah was planning her trip to New York to be with her daughter when a scan revealed that the lung cancer for which she was being treated had spread to her brain. My sister Bala was planning to come to Canberra from Auckland when she died after a lunch with her family and our brother Rajendra from Hamilton. The passing of siblings makes you feel very close to a world that is unravelling, death by death.

Death is: life is?

One sails across the seas of sorrows, always alone. Death is all around us like ashes from bush pyres I see daily these days: trees in flames, the horrors in burnt-out homes and forests. More than human life is disappearing in the summer's season of fires.

*

It was at our sisters' funerals that this book germinated in my mind: certainly the first section. Like blades of grass after the fires, like leaves on broken trees. Things grow between the cracks of one's heart. The questions I was asking, sitting listening to the prayers, mantras, eulogies, hymns, bhajans, consoling words of condolences, handshakes: how does one cope with this fatal reality – so universal yet so personal, so visceral and real that it can so brutally break your heart into pieces and no one even notices a world swiftly passing. You can see your own life mirrored in the sorrows of the world by which we'd built our lives in so many ties of human bondage breaking into bits. The intimations of mortality are most intimate.

Like most men and women, I've lived through great changes and experienced greater beauty and love in my life beyond the biblical age of three score and ten. Jyoti, my beloved since our college days in Delhi, has been a true companion on our many journeys from Fiji to India to England to Australia; to Fiji and India and back, and to elsewhere in the world of our curiosity and quests. We've known immense love and kindness and also coups and migration, loss and displacement. But we've survived with a sense of wholeness for we know we're floating in the cruel seas of life and the splendour in the grass below the sky, breathing. Love, like the wind in blue waves and clouds of illusion, has carried us to many a far country.

Now we're in Canberra: this is our home, finally. I studied here in the 1970s; later my wife and my three children Rohan, Gitanjali and Kavita. Now our granddaughter Hannah Maya, Rohan and Gaby's daughter, is at the ANU. Arjun Sebastian and Kallan Akash, their sons, are not far behind. Only Jesse Arman, Kavita and Michael's son, is in Sydney, where his parents work at two universities. They live close to the Pacific Ocean and feel its golden waves daily as I used to in Fiji walking on the Queen Elizabeth Drive in Suva early every morning.

I mention this because so far we've been lucky by the grace of God: I'm unable to explain this in any other way, having been so close to death, so many times. True, like most people we have experienced the dying of our loved ones in Fiji, India, New Zealand, but they seem to have followed a natural pattern. And the loss of friends and companions in other cities, other countries; death seems a common country without borders.

Every day I see tragedies in the Big Country. Perhaps Death is the biggest country of all. So I thought I'd write my thoughts from my Fijian-Indian experience and see if it gives some understanding to my children when I'm gone. Few people have contemplated more deeply on death and dying than my Indian ancestors. The two epics, the Ramayana and the Mahabharata, explore this reality so imaginatively and philosophically – from the death of a bird to the song celestial of Krishna. It seems fiction alone can help us face this inescapable reality.

On the battlefields of life, worlds are annihilated with a supernal detachment that is superhuman. The merciless epic Mahabharata tells us that in the battle of Kuruchetra eighteen million men died in eighteen days of bitter fighting between cousins. Only a few warrior males survived, including the five Pandava brothers, Krishna, and a handful of others. And a faithful 'dog': dog, god?

It was a hollow victory. The warrior widows, meanwhile, wail and moan as they stream on the battlefield, chasing away the jackals and crows and vultures. The women search for the bodies of their husbands, fathers, sons, brothers.

The Mahabharata is a pitiless epic, a true doomsday book, and we can, in our nuclear age, ignore its dire message only at our peril. The subcontinent is now, it seems, a battlefield of small Kuruchethras, unless Gandhi's message of peace, love and nonviolence is brought into the centre of human vision: all men die, including the Pandavas and their god-guide Krishna.

Life is more relentless: the wonder is that all our wars were envisaged in a single epic, three millennia ago. The holocausts of humanity, oft repeated, but never with the Mahabharata's magnificent magnitude.

Around me the bushfires burn like funeral pyres, destroying all life and human creations. The embers litter the empty roads on which you may see koalas and kangaroos crawling, singed among the charred ruins and twisted iron sheets of homes and once-pristine, tall trees. They speak to us. We are the burnt ones.

*

This book also contains journeys I've made from my little villages in Fiji to the tumultuous city of Delhi, where life and death seem reflected in the ruins of an ancient-modern metropolis; where I found endless love. I've made countless journeys to Delhi – a place in my heart where Ivy, Jyoti's beautiful and loving mother, lived and died. Her love was the most precious gift to us all.

For love alone seems to make me feel that life has been worth living, and once you've known love, you can bear death too. Ivy gave me love I'd not known, a faith I'd not experienced. Today it covers my heart and soul like green ivy leaves spreading on a brick wall of grief; and I think of her often when I see Jyoti's face. One of our daughters is named Kavita Ivy.

Decades ago, I fell in love with a nineteen-year old girl in a Delhi college. This book is a gift to my Jyoti.

1. Leaving

The first day after death, the new absence
Is always the same; we should be careful
Of each other, we should be kind
While there is still time.
– Philip Larkin, 'The Mower'

Dear Jyoti and Satendra

My heart is broken. Bill died, peacefully at the end, but after a lot of suffering, on May 20 at 3 in the afternoon. It was the Monday of a holiday weekend. I was holding his hand and telling him I loved him and goodbye, when he finally stopped breathing . The healthcare worker had just gone out with the garbage to get ready for collection day the next day. I am just so sad. Now I am waiting for various agencies to pick up the wheelchair, bed, etc., and starting all the paperwork. I identified his body at the funeral home yesterday morning. He was wearing a beautiful pale grey wool suit with a white shirt and pale grey silk tie. He will go to be cremated like that. Love, Diana.

Fifteen minutes had barely gone when Jyoti and I talked to our son Rohan, who was driving with his wife Gaby and their two sons, Arjun Sebastian and Kallan Akash, towards their maternal grandmother's farm, a thousand kilometres from Canberra.

Winter morning was warming up.

Then, suddenly, the call, Rohan's voice: 'All's well: we had an accident but no one's hurt.'

Relief but grief simultaneously at what might have happened.

Apparently, a car driven by two youngsters had hit their car at a turning and a wheel had come off Rohan's car. Two seconds more and there could have been fatalities. Luckily, no one was hurt in either car. Some invisible grace, present around us, had saved a family of four and the two young men. They were full of apologies for overtaking a turning vehicle round a corner on a dusty, rural road, with sheep and cattle grazing in the pastures, and farmers arranging their feed on a windy day.

Something that W.H. Auden captured in his poem:

> About suffering they were never wrong,
> ...
> ...how it takes place
> While someone else is eating or opening a window or just walking dully along;
> ...
> Anyhow in a corner, some untidy spot
> Where the dogs go on with their doggy life and the torturer's horse
> Scratches its innocent behind on a tree.
> ...
> And the expensive delicate ship that must have seen
> Something amazing, a boy falling out of the sky,
> Had somewhere to get to and sailed calmly on.

It's a season of drought and dust all around, intensified by the smoke-haze from the wild fires, now burning uncontrollably for months.

The cold on a winter's morning deepened as we waited for our four children to return to Canberra. Life can be as soft as the air we breathe, and as strong as the water we drink. Its randomness is what makes us so human and vulnerable: the more you love, the more you'll suffer, so movingly depicted in the death of Jesus Christ and Mahatma Gandhi. And numerous unremembered ordinary lives.

The cup will not pass.

We drink it daily in our own relationships as family and friends die.

We don't want them to die, but they do, as we will too. We grow towards it from the moment of our birth.

Death is our only certain birthright.

*

So often I've been close to an accident but some mysterious grace has saved my family from fatalities and my driving. I can think of three occasions when I'd have driven into a tragedy but some protecting angel had intervened. Or perhaps the prayers of my ancestors, or someone who loves us. Ivy had taught us how to pray.

Or God's presence in a world so devoid of faith in our comic and cosmic world.

It's about the mystery of the next instant and the unknowable moment of death on which I want to ruminate and write this little book. It happened to me in Fiji Parliament at ten ten a.m. on the morning of 14 May 1987. I'm interjecting: the colonel strides into the modest parliamentary chamber; the ten masked gunmen enter through the low, colonially designed windows. They capture the Prime Minister Dr Timoci Bavadra – we used to call him the healer – and his entire cabinet and government members of the parliament in the Pacific.

Treason at Ten or Darkness at Noon? A whole government abducted at gunpoint from inside the parliamentary chambers and incarcerated for almost a week in two separate places: separating Fijians from Indians. This in little Fiji: the paradise of the South Pacific, where people had not heard of a coup or knew how to spell the ghastly word.

I've written a version of it in my two books *The Wounded Sea* and *1987 – Six Nights in May*. Today, on the fiftieth anniversary of Fiji's independence, Fiji is groggily waking up from that terrible nightmare.

Life has never been the same for my small country and my small family. And for thousands of others who were compelled to leave the country of their birth by the brutal betrayal of a colonel and the Royal Fiji Military Forces, hitherto unknown in the islands of the South Seas.

And the silences of so many Pacific Islanders who saw 'Indians' as aliens in an ocean in which so many seas mixed.

Paradises are lost in an instant like the lives of those we love. But an instant can haunt you forever, depending on what it contains.

*

I write this with my limited knowledge and understanding of how we cope with grief which can touch us in the trembling of a leaf. Every day we see incredible tragedies on television, hear on the radio and read in the daily newspapers: the dying of a mother with four children in a car crash, the stabbing of a man by another man, the killing of a woman, the drowning of children, the death of refugees in a boat, asylum seekers asphyxiated in a lorry, soldiers dying in the desert sands; bombs blowing up old ruins and new buildings; an avalanche slides down a slope, and two young sons are buried beneath it as two parents come down to see if their two sons are safe. And the dying in droughts, famine, flood, fires and those sinking boats in the seas and the plane crashes on the earth. The mindless acts of terrorism: the terror and the pity of it all. Who can ever forget the killings in Christchurch mosques. And all that happens in hospitals and hospices, in the eruptions of volcanoes and the shaking of our earth.

Covid-19 is a curse of unprecedented proportions defining human fate. And our helpless vulnerability.

In the old days, the old were not that old. Perhaps they saw less and experienced more.

Death is as endless as life. Grief is a sea without shores: it's a country in our hearts without borders. Suffering seems the unalterable condition of our being: so much blood and pain at birth as if one's future is foretold in one's mother's birth pangs.

Ask not for whom the bells toll…

Death is all around us, so is life: in my garden, planted by the previous owners of this modest home we call ours, three daffodils have suddenly bloomed, raising their golden heads above dried grass and fallen leaves of winter's withering, reminding me of my three grandsons… two blackbirds have built their precarious nest on a green, leafy tree. Every morning is a parrot-coloured dawn among a row of white roses shimmering in the sunlight after a misty morning.

Last year in three months I lost two sisters, one aged eighty, the other eighty-two; one in Bangalore, the other in Auckland. Sheilah, my wife Jyoti's sister, was born in New Delhi; Bala, my sister, in Nadi. Both were our, Jyoti's and mine, older sisters.

We attended both funerals. I had also attended their weddings: one in an obscure village in Fiji; the other in the heart of Nehru's New Delhi on Akbar Road.

Their lives were different: one an accomplished pianist, trained in London; the other a peasant woman with barely a few years of primary schooling. One migrated from Delhi to Bangalore; the other from Nadi to Auckland. One's ancestors had never left Rajasthan; the other's had left the United Provinces of British India at the turn of the nineteenth century and never returned.

Generations were born and bred on the islands. Fiji was home.

My sister-in-law Sheilah was a well-travelled woman, married to an extraordinarily talented man. They had travelled and lived overseas as Rana was the chairman of a multinational firm run by Indians and Swiss. I'd lived with them in Juhu Beach in Bombay. My brother, Dr Davendra Nandan, visited them often while studying in Bombay for his medical degree.

My sister, Shiv Kumari, married young and had four children. They were poor peasants in Natawa, Tavua. The year when I left for Delhi to study on a small scholarship, my brother-in-law Ram was struck by polio. When I returned, we persuaded our father in Lega Lega, Nadi, to give a portion of our farmland to Bala. My father did precisely that and her three children, Premila, Pramod, Sushma, began going to school. Vinod worked on the farm as a canecutter.

Today, my sister's children are in Auckland: Premila and her husband with a large family, Sushma and Navin, both doctors, and Pramod and Sunita, with their children and grandchildren, and Pramod with a PhD. As I write this, all are travelling in India.

At my widowed sister's funeral, I saw the family from Fiji: they had all migrated to perhaps the most multicultural city in the South Pacific, Auckland. It was a revelation for I met people Jyoti and I hadn't seen for years.

Migration, I'd written, in my poem 'Lines Across Black Waters', is transmigration. I have often wondered if those who haven't migrated or have never been forced to migrate can even imagine the crippling sorrow of people who leave the places of their birth and are compelled to find other homes for they have been exiled so often against their will. Many Fiji Indians have had to share that fate. And it's my generation, born during the Second World War, that suffered this terrible tryst with destiny because of the treacherous acts of a trusted colonel. The sorrows of migration are many and they keep haunting our lives like waves breaking on half-submerged rocks in a sea.

I'm aware that we're comparatively lucky, compared to the fate of many refugees and migrants from many other parts of our increasingly broken world. We have Australasia: Fiji, Australia, New Zealand is our special region, physically and imaginatively. So many of my relatives now work in the islands of the South Pacific. And of course in Australia and New Zealand.

We can call our tragic misfortune a fortunate piece of luck. Fijians generally make peaceful, self-respecting citizens. My semi-literate sister was able to give her children and grandchildren a life that I couldn't have imagined forty years ago.

These thoughts came to my mind as I spoke at her funeral. But the grief persists for a lost world and the minutiae of life by which we live, love and learn to forgive: the bures, trees, stones, rivers, sugar cane fields, the vegetable gardens, the one cow that we milked early morning as the sun rose over the hills, the darba in which the single cock crowed to see the sun; and that early morning bowl of tea under the mango or tamarind tree or that flamboyant flaming not far from the well, often full of frogs. And that starry sky at night.

The habitus of a childhood home is irreplaceable.

And that vanishing generation: nana-nani, aja-aji.

At midday, your grandfather lying under a tree, planted by his dead wife, dreaming of youth and age, or the home he'd left behind in that mystic land he called his mulk. We never discovered their mystery and they never spoke about that other life: the other side of silence. We were, like their children, born on one island. That was our world. History's cruelty and cunning hadn't meant much to me. Ignorance was truly blissful.

Yet today I think of them together. Death, the great leveller, is also the great democrat. All may not be created equal, but we all die equally, universally. And are cremated equally.

In death's kingdom, we're equal citizens. There's a place for everyone, everywhere.

*

This is the story of my attempts at coping with loss and grief at my age. But I've written it for those who may live long after I'm gone. I'm now in the frontline, as one of my brothers put it at my sister's funeral in Auckland, with a twinkle in his sad eyes, for he comes after me. And at every funeral we're reminded of our own intimations of mortality. We wonder who will go first. We always mourn for our death at any dying.

We were seven: now we are four.

I've written a number of obituaries: from the death of Pandit Nehru to Dr Timoci Bavadra, the deposed prime minister of Fiji; and Gough Whitlam, the dismissed prime minister of Australia.

I've written at the death of Indira Gandhi and Rajiv Gandhi – it was my way of honouring them, for in strange ways they had touched my life with their words and greetings.

I've also given eulogies at the death of friends and relatives, even strangers, for this is a politician's hazard in a place like Fiji. Many survived by giving funeral orations.

Or wedding speeches, after a long wedding ceremony. The last one I gave was in Auckland in March 2019.

*

The death of one's grandparents is in the natural order of things: the first death I remember is that of my paternal grandfather, my ancient-looking aja with ashen wisps of hair on his Gandhi-like skull, who died suddenly in Lautoka hospital one night. My father had rushed him there on his old Ferguson tractor. When he returned, around midnight, he went to my aja's broken bure, sat on the empty plass and wailed.

I'd no idea of his age, or his illness. People were born, lived and died, especially if they had come from India. Today their silence is most hauntingly heard in the rippling sea of memory.

My father's father, who lived with him and seemed immortal for he was from India, had died. Villagers began arriving after midnight; and the pounding of kava began: it was a consoling sound, so common in my tawdry village, Leg Lega, by the Nadi international airport. The planes seem to come and go from nowhere to nowhere. Our life, like the small river with tiny waves, flowed quietly forever, stippling the edges of the green grass on which cows grazed to give us milk. Relatives we knew died in remote villages on the island but it's really the death of my father that touched me most deeply, when an awareness of death came to into my consciousness with a searing force.

I'd envisioned the death of my father in my poem 'My Father's Son' in 1975 after his almost fatal stroke; after it, he never spoke a word; and finally died in 1978.

In September 1975, seeing my father lying on a steel bed in Lautoka Hospital was truly heartbreaking. My young brother hurried home from Grant's Medical College in Bombay.

I returned to Canberra and wrote this piece, first published in *PIM*, the *Pacific Islands Monthly*, when death came so close to me, though my father was still alive, looked after by my brother Davendra and his wife Saras, both doctors.

My Father's Son

The airport, metallic, tarred,
Rising from the deep, blue sea;
A white watch tower erect
Watching darkly;
Jumbos idle like oiled white bodies
On the beach;
While sea-fishes feed to be fed.
A few hotels on the landscape –
Bruises on the peasant face.
The village – dark and dumb
So sullen in the sun;
A muddy lost track
Hobbles to a hut on the hill.

A red hill with four coconut trees;
Under the mango tree a dozen goats
A red flag withered and holy
Burnt in the sun,
Children – naked, ribs dancing in the light,
Teeth beaming with stolen sugarcane,
Growing with minah birds.

Below the hill, a well
Full of frogs
Two boys and a girl
Shrieking with killing stones:
Four frogs are floating,
Their white bellies up,
Eyes to the sun.
Children had their fun.

Quiet and ageless as the hill
The old man comes with a lathi:
A sudden slap, a scream: I run.
He curses my mother,
Pulls them out one by one
For the red, griefless earth.
The cow grazes and gazes
And moos for a second birth.

II
That was years ago,
I was young and unkind –
To the frogs, I mean.

Now in this conditioned office
On a swivel chair and putrid air
I batten on –
Defined, secure in a sinecure.
I see the island in the sea
Where my father was quarantined:
'For two weeks only,' he said.
'But the journey?' I asked.

His eyes withdrew into himself:
'The dark waters, the blind winds,
The landless sea forever raging.
It was narak; many died; I survived.
What retribution for leaving a loving home
And the cows grazing beside a mandir
My friends playing gullidanda.
Sleeping and eating we arrived.'

That's how he remembered
The passage of one life into another.

III
Early morning – rain, rain, rain.
The phone rang: wrong number,
I yawned.
My brother simply said
'Pitaji's dead.'

Oh, I'll forgo the dinner.
Death comes without invitation;
Worse such dinners are so rare
With the satrap's wife
With so promiscuous an air.

The old village was there
In the old man's bure:
A tattered mat on a three-legged 'bed'
The black blanket
That had made my childhood so warm
The ubiquitous mosquito net
With numerous knots and patches.
Near the tanoa sat the frog
Eyes bulging, ineluctable as ever.
The tanoa was empty
But the smell of grog was in the corner
Where I used to serve the taukei.

The village was there
Toothless, faceless, nameless, landless
Except old Pookladdu, the peasant politician,
And Buddhu the pujari
Who burnt himself fire-walking
(How Father had laughed!)
And wanted to lift the hill like Hanuman.
Others heads grown grey
Hearts grown old
A hundred years
In a hundred wrinkles.
I looked too well-fed, mumbled 'RamRam'
And sank into the only chair.

And saw his ribs rippling;
His grotesque loincloth like Christ's.
I wondered if he, too, had paid the price
For his children's children?
They said there's no need to weep
He died in his sleep
He was so old – no one knew his age;
Besides, he had to go –
His land, on which his wife was buried,
Was 'reserved' two weeks ago.

In the children, the parents live again.

They washed the dead old man
I poured a lotah of water
But around me there was only death and decay
There were flies round the corners of his eyes.

Next to the airport there's a crematorium
Built by a shopkeeper for his drowned son
(Or was it for an election he never won?)
The pandit gave a speech
Read a few mantras from a red book
Blessed us all with the dead;
Which neither the living nor the dead understood;
They poured 'pure Australian ghee'
From a Fiji Bitter bottle.
My brother lit the pyre
While I stood looking out at the sea.

In an hour – ashes to ashes.

Thank god it didn't rain.
Oum Shantih, Shantih, Shantih.

IV
The sea beat against the shore
With the monotony of the human heart
The sun sank in the ocean
Like a shark;
The sky was a mutilated hibiscus
Around me all was dark.
I sat on the beach till the spittle
Of the ocean touched my feet
And I flew to my retreat.

It's different here:
I see the island
Touched by a rainbow, a yacht,
And a black minah bird.

*

Decades later, after the two Fijian coups, when I was in Canberra, my mother passed away. Both my parents died in my doctor brother's home, one in the village of Lega Lega, the other in the heart of the one-street Nadi town. It's some consolation to know your parents were given the best medicine and the best care in their fragile, mortal condition.

It's my mother's death that made me write my first serious article on death and dying. A version was published in *Meanjin*.

'The Sea is One'

We return often to our place of birth, even if it's only to attend a funeral. Yesterday I was back in Fiji, my special piece of earth, to cremate my mother's body and perform the antyesti samskara, the Hindu funeral ceremonies.

Of course one never returns to the same place – spaces change, there are new people occupying your old houses, different and indifferent neighbours. You, too, have altered your estate and memory plays its own tricks. The wholeness can never be repossessed for the dispossessed, and yet you long for the paradise that never was or will be. The present is your postcard of pain, of loss and relics. Everyone, it seemed, had been waiting for us, especially me – I'm the child furthest away from my mother and my motherland. Canberra adds it own distances to abandoned places, dislocated lives among transplanted trees.

I'd talked to my mother on Sunday – she sounded well, her voice whole. It gave me a lot of peace of mind to talk to my mother virtually every weekend. Our conversations were brief.

'How're you, mum?'

She'd reply in broken sentences understanding some of the English words that came out naturally from me. My mother knew no English – I listened and breathed it daily.

I'd make a few routine inquiries about my elder brother and my elder sister and their family. Then I'd put the phone down, knowing my brother and his wife, both doctors, were giving her the best of care.

On Tuesday at nine fifteen p.m., I get a call from my other brother in Auckland. Mother had passed away at seven twenty p.m.

'Passed away' conveyed an expected death. We'd planned to see her in September. My first concerns are to make arrangements to fly to Fiji. But tomorrow there are no flights from Sydney to Nadi. Jyoti and our daughters sit by my side on the bed. Rohan, our son, comes from his house. There's a cold sadness spreading from room to room. It's winter here. Looking at Jyoti's face and my children's, I sense the deeper suffering of my mother.

You can bury the griefs of your parents; how does one bear the sorrows of one's children?

My mother was not an articulate woman. She spoke in her silences and acts of affections. Like so many women of her generation in Fiji, she lived in her children. How can I ever forget her image in widow-white framed in the doorway waving goodbye to me, my wife and my daughters, Gita and Kavita, on 3 December 1987, as we left my brother's home to come to Canberra for a few months, away from the evil that I felt was infecting Fiji after the coups. We stayed on in this migrant city of rolling hills, ghostly gums and little lakes.

Next morning, the grizzled stubble on my chin is like my lawn, grey with frost. But preparations for this journey have to be made. Travel plans to funeral keep one's mind off the unimaginable absences that could fever your brain or break the heart.

After that December morning in 1987, I had gone back to Fiji after five years, three months and eight days later. My wife and children never saw my mother alive again. Now all had come to her funeral. Rohan, the eldest, had returned after almost eleven years. He had never been to this home where my mother had died. In her death, she'd brought us together under one roof, with relatives from other cities and countries. We were the last to arrive. My mother had known only one country, Fiji. She'd died eight kilometres from her place of birth; and five kilometres away she was to be cremated that afternoon. On Wailoaloa Beach crematorium.

*

I grew up in the village with a delightful mess of marriages, and with the gaiety of festivals

Ramleela, Diwali, Holi and the grief of funerals. Death was part of our lives. The last family funeral I'd attended was my father's, eighteen years ago in 1978. But my mother's funeral was being held in Nadi town, the streets of which I had walked barefooted, holding her sari, from shop to shop to buy the cheapest garments. The town had been transformed. The timber, single-storey buildings had given way to three-storey concrete blocks. Instead of farmers on horseback, we now had colourful vans and coaches, taxi drivers and young businessmen, selling some of the most curious handicrafts to sunburnt tourists.

At my mother's funeral, there're only muffled sounds. Sorrow is subdued. I see my brothers and sisters, grey men and women, their wives and husbands, their strong sons and daughters, all with tearful faces. The coffin lies upstairs.

I look at my mother's serene and lovely face. Her lips are open and two of her beautiful teeth are visible. The mouth is a wound that even death will not heal. I touch her face and touch my forehead. My children simply stare at their dead grandmother, now confined to a rough-hewn, wooden, crudely varnished coffin box. She is covered in a pure white kaffan (cotton shroud).

I greet many faces, people I haven't seen since the day I'd flown to India to study, almost forty years ago. Life's trajectory had taken me in other directions, to other destinations, to a deracinated destiny. And here at my mother's funeral, I was seeing, as if for the first time, the people in whose lives I'd grown, in whose thatched houses I'd spent my childhood and a part of my youth. My older cousins and their relatives had come from Votualevu, LegaLega, Nasua, Sablau, Maigania, Korovuto, Tunalia, TagiTagi…places in my heart.

The coffin is brought downstairs – there's more space here. Men and women go round the coffin with folded palms, pay their last respects as the pandit keeps mumbling the mantras which I scarcely understand. But understanding of words in death is not necessary. Just as well. For if one could understand death, how terrible living would be. I know whatever is being chanted, it gives solace to the living. It gives a final grace to my mother's last journey.

For me it was quietly moving, the mantras, the prayers and these women and men seeing on my mother's dead face the intimations of their own mortality. Then they sit down on mats and paals sewn out of sugar sacks. Some men keep standing on the edges of the garden full of green tropical plants and flowers my sister-in-law has lovingly planted. Gardening, she'd said, is so healing. There are lots of flowers for my mother's funeral rituals. I cannot name them, these brilliantly coloured petals I hold in the palm of my right hand.

The pandit, a young man in his thirties, in his pink cotton shirt and brown terylene trousers, begins the ceremonies. At my father's funeral, the pandit was an older person from our village – he must have worn a dhoti and a white kurta and recited the mantras from his memory, holding a red, tattered Sanskrit book, probably a version of the Ramayana. This younger priest begins by reading in Hindi a chapter of the Bhagwad Gita, perhaps our world's most celestial poem about death, about the transcendent soul, about the cessation of birth itself. Unlike many other scriptures, where birth after death is important, the quintessential teaching of the Gita is how to end the cycle of recurring births. Rebirth is the reason for all our suffering.

The Gita has become the foundational text of Hinduism, a beautiful poem embalmed as sacred text like the Bible or the Koran. Hinduism, too, needs its prophets and its sacred texts. From the deserts the prophets came and from the prophets the deserts and profits, whispers my sceptical mind! The Gita is interpolated in the world's longest poem, the Mahabharata, an epic of moral chaos both within the individual and outside, where dharma has been ruthlessly damaged by Duruyodhana, the blind king Dhristirashtra's demonic son.

*

It is difficult to sit on the floor for more than an hour. The modern pandit senses our discomfort and finishes the Gitapath after two chapters. One by one, my brothers, our wives and sisters are called by him near my mother's body. We dip a mango leaf in a glass of water and let the glistening drops roll into my mother's mouth. All her children perform this post-mortem sacrament. The pandit shows his slight disappointment with my gestures – I've not let the drops from the green leaf trickle into my mother's mouth, instead they roll down her right cheek like tears breaking. One of my sisters notices this clumsiness and smiles indulgently as my mother would have.

Then the speeches begin, first from the pandit – he emphasises my mother's inclinations, in her old age, towards Hindu holiness. A businessman, a Sikh, who has known the family from our childhood, talks eloquently about a mother, quoting from his sacred text. Then the former headmaster of our primary school, where my brothers and I had studied, tells of my mother's love for her children's education.

Listening to all this, my brother's son Rakesh asks me to say a few words on behalf of the family. This is normally not done: at a funeral, others speak on behalf of the family. I can barely utter a few words but in the pocket of my blue jeans I've a copy of my poem 'Siddharth', written in 1978, when, on my return from Australia, I saw my father dying in the village in his home where my youngest brother was now living. Both he and his wife had returned as doctors – they had a three-year-old son named Siddharth, now standing tall behind me watching intently.

The scene of my father dying in one room and little Siddharth playing in another room next to it, had brought in me a new awareness of life. It reminded me of young Siddharth, the Buddha's other name, who leaves his kingdom, his wife and child at the midnight hour to go in search of an answer to human sorrow, the greatest of which is death. He was twenty-nine years old. I had a vague idea of how he became the Light of Asia.

I take out my poem, a Hindi translation. My father had died aged sixty-five; my mother died at eighty-one. And all their children are alive; there's gladness in that thought. I do not say much but read the poem, for I want my mother and father remembered together in their death. In life, they might have been separated in body, in love, in those little denials and disappointments that all living flesh is heir to. In their death, I wanted to imagine and remember they were undivided. In death, so much we thought important in life is so insignificant, yet so immeasurable. So I read.

Siddharth

Day by day, cell by cell,
Between the silences
In drops of blood.
The hibiscus blooms
Beyond desire;
We live from moment to moment
On the faith of maya.

Rays of a sinking sun splinter the sea.
Twilight brightens another sky;
My father is dying;
No, not I.
A foetus tied in
Strings of sorrow –
What womb dare hold him
now?
The earth –
The first, the last mother.
There's no pain like this body
Nor no life like this death
The endless apotheosis
Of all living;
Arjuna's vision in Krishna

The nuclear fission of an atman:
Of darkness or illumination?

I cannot say.
The dying man will not tell.
Draw the curtain
Eyelids flicker…
Faces light up the landscape
Through battered hills, broken trees;
Men, women behind the chariot wheels,
Glow like memory-motes
In the last rays
Of a Kuruchetra sun.
A tear blinds the third eye;
The sea is broken by bits of rain.
Now all sorrows surcease:

'Waves are nothing but water.
So is the sea.'

II
Rain falls on dry grass
The earth's smell fill the air
Stones stir with drops
Voices tumble over dark waters
Waves become whales
In dry coconut skulls!
The Nandi floods again;
Pandit has lopped Lali's tail
And I haven't even learnt to swim!
Siddharth, my son, my father
Eyes lit with another life:
Of the Four Sights you've seen two

In your father's father:
A sick man, an old one, too.

The third they'll not let you see
A corpse cleaned like a salt-fish,
Powdered, scented, tinted
With marigolds, hibiscus petals
Burnt on the seasand
A mutthi of ashes
Enough for his roti.

Ants crawl on living stones
Worms live in the marrow of our bones.
The fourth, a monk, you may yet
become:
To know the helpless endlessness of
our being.
No old paths lead to that
knowledge
No other footfalls are
heard
Nor even the sound of a tiny bird
Chirping the mantras of dead men:
'Oum! Amen! Shantih!'

Siddharth, once again,
Follow your own footsteps
Over ashes and blades of
grass
And teach us to live.
In life, from Life!

   This gesture is unusual. The pandit wants the poem and chants a few farewell mantras. The coffin is lifted and carried by us, brothers and cousins, and loaded into a van. There's no wailing. My mausi, my mother's only surviving elder sister, weeps uncontrollably.

*

We drive from my brother's home towards the Wailoaloa beach where, on the edge of the Pacific Ocean, is the cremation site. It's been there since my childhood days, when the dread of death was so close, yet so distant. We were both fascinated and frightened by the fire of the pyre. My father's funeral was far from our village. It was a longer journey in old cars and cargo lorries. From my brother's, the cremation ground appears nearer perhaps because the roads are better and we all travel by Japanese cars from the town. Through Sagayam Road, we enter the main street of Nadi town. It's three p.m. and the town is bursting with schoolchildren. We turn left and cross the Nadi Bridge into Namotomoto koro, the native village on the bank of the Nadi river as naturally part of the earth as the river itself.

But the river has changed its course.

I recall the days when there was the wooden bridge that was broken and washed away in every flood and we'd use little boats, rowed by young Fijians from the koro, to cross the flooded river to the school – a couple of corrugated-iron sheds on the other side, in the shadow of the Sangam temple, decorated by gaudy and garish paintings of gods, goddesses and a multicoloured peacock. The bridge now is made of concrete, the temple is built on a safer ground and is called the SriSubramanyam Temple – a video vision of it is shown on our flight to Nadi from Sydney by Air Pacific. The Vivekananda High School shifted years ago to higher ground in Malolo. Only Swamiji's ashram is near the bridge and both Swamiji, the founder, and Mr P.N. D. Moosad, the principal, are dead. A whole world like a fast forward film flits across my mind's eye as I sit near the coffin in the van, rattling over the bridge.

A world had vanished and, in my many flights from Nadi airport, I'd scarcely noticed it.

*

One evening, almost forty years ago, my mother, my father, my mausi and I sat on wooden chairs on the concrete floor of the school. It was an evening of prize-giving. I had, in my Senior Cambridge class that year, won several prizes including the Principal's Prize and a 'gold medal' for a Hindi essay. My parents had sat through the speeches in English, especially the longest one by Swamiji, and Principal Moosad's annual report and prizes for every class – first, second and third – until at last it was my turn to receive my prizes in the senior-most form.

In the evening darkness, I did not see my parents' faces, nor was I very keen to show the smart boys and girls of the town who my parents were. As soon as the ceremony was over, my proud father hired a taxi from the town to our village home. It was the first time I rode in a taxi with my parents. Two days later, my mother persuaded my father to buy me my first pair of shoes of which I wrote in my first short story, 'A Pair of Black Shoes', now a popular piece of fiction in Fiji's secondary schools.

Namotomoto village now has concrete houses. One doesn't hear the carefree laughter of the Fijians much these days. No one swims in the river or waves or shouts with joy at passing cars or school buses. Not far from the village are Fiji's famous hotels, Sheraton and Regent, presumably now owned by Japanese and Malaysian corporations. Across the road are Korean warehouses and Chinese shops. Prosperity is nibbling at the edges of the Fijian village.

Men and women, in the acrid light of the afternoon sun, pause briefly to look at the funeral procession. Beyond the Kennedy Avenue, Nadi's prestigious residential suburb, we reach Enamanu Road, opposite Saunaka village. We turn left into Enamanu Road. I'm astounded to see a McDonald's on the right, full of excited schoolchildren.

On the dusty, bumpy road across farms and small houses, a pastoral scene desiccated by sugar cane, with curious women pausing in their work to stare at us, we reach the edge of the sea, reflecting death's infinity. It is from here we used to get fresh fish for our dinner in the village. We turn left. One kilometre away I see the corrugated tin shed standing on rusted steel posts in the shadow of a few barren palms. The sea spray has eaten the steel like cancer in a body. The radio must have announced my mother's funeral at three p.m. – already a crowd is there. Since early morning, my sister's son, Vinod, the farmer and cane-cutter, has been building the funeral pyre for his nani just outside the shed.

I see this as the most beautiful setting for a crematorium in the world. The sea beats against the shore with the monotony of the human heart. And like my mother, through the tangled thicket of life, we, one by one, reach the shore to see the unknown endlessness that lies beyond, in the mystery of water that connects everything, except that this sea is my wounded sea.

Once again, the pandit takes over. My youngest brother wraps a white cloth sulu-like round his waist. The body of my mother is removed from the coffin box. Six of us lift it and place it on the pyre and look at the intricate artifice by which the pyre has been constructed, log by log. My Indian-born grandparents were cremated with doqo logs. During my father's funeral, we'd used tiritiri logs. My mother's pyre is made of pine wood.

I look at my mother's body, wrapped in a new white shroud, as it lies on these dead logs. My youngest brother's face is ashen, grief-stricken. The youngest has borne the most – the caring and the dying of our parents. He has to light this pile of wood, too. My mother had given birth to seven children, five boys, two girls, and had had several miscarriages. Her children and grandchildren were still struggling for their rights in their parents' country of birth. And now here she was, frail and flammable, just bones held together by skin, and her the prana, breath of life, gone. Why should the sea be so alive? And your mother so dead?

Gently we place logs over her body, every log heavier than the corpse, I feel. I'd seen my wife, my children and my brothers and sisters weep softly. Now suddenly I feel my heart will break. This grief coiled inside me must find some utterance. But no tears fall from my eyes.

Again I hear the pandit's mantras, incantations of death mingling with the aroma of ghee, camphor and rice burning the minutiae of the offerings and oblations bless the dead; they seem essential to any Hindu rites of passage. This journey, unlike any other, was from one world to another. And the traveller had to be meticulously prepared for she now was going it alone. My brother walks round the pyre lighting it at several places. We, too, place lit camphors in the pyre. It burns, crackles, flames and leaps into the setting sun. The terrible beauty of a burning pyre against the blue waves, green fields.

We sit by the pyre, our faces lit by its haunting light. The corpse-consuming fire, the ship-eating sea. The terror of cremation or the sacred act of transmigration? This, I sense, is the explosion of the soul not mentioned in the Gita. That darkness in the heart of light which makes God a necessity to help us bear the unbearable.

*

One by one our friends and relatives leave. They had paid their respects. We must bear our sorrows ourselves. As the pyre glows, an Air Pacific jet lands at the Nadi airport – a flight from Sydney. Everything else is so quiet on the shore of this beautiful and savage sea. The sea's surface has a numinous glow, the flames from the pyre make the ripples radiant. I sit with my brothers looking at the glowing, dying pyre. The fire's insatiable appetite fed on my mother's flesh too. There's an eerie melancholy about the evening. Grief, like blood on a white sheet from small wounds bleeding slowly, seems to be spreading across the ocean. Only the incandescent pyre creates a circle of light. Tired by life, defeated by death, we too decide to drive home for a cup of tea.

We return as the sun has sunk into the waves. In the gathering darkness, a part of the sky is ablaze. It's a tropical sunset in its many hues, a scene I'd almost forgotten. The colours here are sharp and brilliant and below, the silent sea heaves, pulsates, breathes, like a woman heavy with another child walking up the hill. A faraway tide is lapping the shore, and darkness, like a primordial bird, spreads its wings upon the face of the deep. We park the car with the headlights on. Two of us walk to the pyre, where a few logs have fallen. We rearrange them again. The embers are glowing, bright and beautiful, as so many memories of my burnt-out mother harrow my heart shaking with unshed tears.

We come home, where my mother had lived her last days. Her room is empty except for the pictures of Hindu gods and goddesses. Sai Baba blesses all in saffron robe and hair like an indigenous chief's. And there's a huge picture of a fluffy, adorable cat on the top left hand corner of the wall, above all the deities. My mother must have prayed to the cat, too.

Upstairs in the kitchen, the women are making tea; the men are mixing yagona downstairs. We sit downstairs, the same place where a few hours ago we'd sanctified our mother's body with alien, ancient mantras. We tell jokes to each other and I'm astonished how soon life and laughter take over. It's the most magical and miraculous transformation. One feels grateful for that. And I'm glad my brothers have a sense of laughter about them. I find this exhilarating – this is death and the whole truth.

My youngest brother, the one who last saw my mother alive twenty minutes before she died, tells his many jokes.

Thus the evening passed with migrant jokes and indigenous yaqona. It's been a long day's journey into the night and some of us sleep on the floor.

*

At the death of one's last parent there's a sense of finality in this loss, as if the last link is being broken from a world you've known so intimately. After all, one's childhood is one's most authentic history. And if you've been in exile, the loss is all the more felt for you'll not hear the voice of your mother again. Your mother tongue is replaced by another language, in another landscape. The sounds are different, the thoughts distant. And the songs of your childhood are no more the songs of your children.

But this death also brings a sense of liberation. You feel freer, as if the last burden has been lifted from your heart. The umbilical attachment has finally fallen off.

The pleasures of exile, the notes of banishment, are central to the two Indian epics the Ramayana and the Mahabharata. My mother used to tell us stories from these books. Sleeping on her plaas, made of dried grass sewn in the CSR company's stolen sugar sacks, covered by a Fijian mat, we lay on either side of her listening to these great and glorious stories from India. My mother could read Hindi, so she'd read Hindi magazines and detective stories, jaasoosikahani, brought to our home by a man from Lautoka named Mama Lal Singh. Then she'd retell them to her children, jumbled together. We'd neither radio nor television but we'd plenty of time for stories, an ocean of ancient tales, and because they were from India, they were truly real, we thought.

I see the faces from so many villages, villagers among whom I'd spent such a large part of my childhood and early youth and had titled my first book of poems *Faces in a Village*. Suddenly, seeing these withered, wrinkled men and women, I realised the sources from where the little streams of life had flowed into my mother. I was glad my children who had been oblivious of this part of my origin were there, seeing the hidden history of their father, the subterranean sources of his being. My mother had held them like a thread in a garland. I do not think I'll ever attend a funeral like that again.

In the Mahabharata, there's a wonderful couplet about the origins of human beings. One is not rooted like a tree in a landscape – the human spirit is more like a river, ever-flowing, ever-changing, ever renewing itself and always moving to join the indivisible ocean. But more significantly if one were to search for the source of a river, one would find not a single spring that gives it life but myriads of them. So are the beginnings of human beings. They are shaped by innumerable sources, and in our blood and bones, brains and veins, we carry the memories and minerals of so many, dead and living and yet unborn.

My brothers and I walk on the beach, once again, trampling on seashells. How deeply this land had shaped my life, I begin to sense only when the last embers of my mother's funeral pyre are turning into ashes. I find no solace in the lines:

> It is, therefore, a source of great virtue for the practised mind to learn, bit by bit, first to change about in visible and transitory things, so that afterwards it may be able to leave them behind altogether. The person who finds his homeland sweet is still a tender beginner; he to whom every soil is as his native one is already strong; but he is perfect to whom the entire world is as a foreign place. The tender soul has fixed his love on one spot in the world; the strong person has extended his love to all places; the perfect man has extinguished his.

The dying embers have ignited a new passion in my heart, a sorrow deeper than the sea on whose shore I can no longer weep.

*

A day passes sadly, slowly. Next morning, we go with the pandit to the cremation ground to collect my mother's splintered bones from the ashes and cast them into the sea. The sun is sharp like a shark's fin. Life on the street is normal. There's no sign of death, except perhaps in a handful of hearts. We drive to the Wailoaloa beach. A few tourists are taking their morning walk from the nearby motels. They see our cars and wave, cameras clicking.

The cremation spot has been thoroughly swept and cleaned by my cousin, Ram Narayan, except for the ashes in the pyre square. Bent, we search for pieces of bones among them. I can show you fear in a fistful of dust – I begin to understand the line. It is ashes to ashes, always. My son stands at a distance. My brothers and I rake the cold ashes with our fingers and collect every bit of bone, our mother's, in a new white cloth.

The pandit begins chanting as soon as he sees we've collected the bones of the cremated. My youngest brother takes off his trousers and shirt, wraps a white sulu-dhoti round his waist, stands bare-chested, with the bones, and after the pandit's mantras have sanctified the bones, he walks into the sea, the deeper the better. His broad shoulders heavy in the saltwater sun; his handsome face, our parents' gift, so sorrowful. With the bundle of bones, he sinks into the waves for a minute and rises without it and returns to the shore.

The bones are now part of the ocean, part of the sand and seashells and will mingle with the waters of the Ganges, though the Nandi was closer to my mother's bones. An unanchored soul had been finally anchored, or so we consoled ourselves.

There's a flight of birds and the tourists are watching them disappear into the blue haze of the igneous mountains to the right. As we return to collect our things on the sand, a van arrives with four men to prepare a new pyre for another funeral. It's a farmer's from Togo. His ashes will mingle with my mother's as my mother's have with a thousand others. I know my mother would have recognised his name for she used to listen to the death notices on the radio so attentively.

These men, pyre-makers, who I do not know, shake my hand and my brothers' with the recognition of strangers who, however briefly, share some common knowledge and become aware of a fatal, binding truth.

Not far from the cremation ground, a large boat is stranded on the sands. I take a picture of *Adi Litia*, tilted and deserted, sandcrabs scuttling around it and a few mynah birds chirping on its broken rusting bow.

*

One had grown with death all around in the village. Old indentured labourers were dying and their cremations took place on the Wailoaloa beach, next to it the cemetery for burials. Some were buried on the hills surrounded by the canefields. On their graves, cows grazed, and an occasional pandanus tree grew. We were afraid to sit under it when the wind suddenly rose. And leaves quivered in the midday heat. But death was a remote reality; they were all our aja-aji, nananani. We were related in a common kinship that the jehajibhais and jahajins had created across the seven seas, travelling in the same boats.

These deaths so common didn't touch me in any significant way. We'd accepted dying as part of life and living. The dead were cremated on the shores of the largest ocean as if a wave had reached its destination, born out of the womb of the ocean; new waves would endlessly be born. We kept playing our gullidanda and goli on the ground they had walked on, or sat under the tamarind or mango tree on a hot day, dreaming of past life or the coming of death, as brightness fell from the tropical sun. And rain slashed their fields.

They didn't say much: their birthplaces were thousands of miles away.

Mortality and old age were for others. No, not us.

The miracle was that we heard death notices on the radio, on the village coconut wireless but we never felt that death would confront us or our family.

Get me a mustard seed, the Buddha said to the grieving woman searching for an answer for a death in her family, from a home death has not visited. She went from hut to hut, palace to palace, and returned to the Enlightened One under the lonely tree and simply said, Now I understand.

Death is universal. All art, all life is created to understand this fatal reality which can come at any moment to anyone. It's one transcendent truth.

A man died in your village or in the next one. The word spread and children remained indoors, scared of ghosts and tivoros.

Dead bodies were taken to the shabby cremation ground on the beach. The pandit performed the rituals; the oldest child, a son, lit the pyre. The burning pyre in the evening had a strange fascination for us. Fear came only in the dark.

During my childhood and youth, women seldom attended the burning of the pyre.

It burnt out in a few hours and we returned home. No cooking was done for several days: the neighbours and relatives brought cooked food and lots of tea with plenty of sugar. Sugar was never in short supply thanks to the Oz CSR company which had recruited many of these men and women to work on the sugar estates it owned on the fertile, volcanic islands.

My grandparents like thousands of others had placed their left thumb mark on a piece of paper – an agreement was signed and sealed in Calcutta. They had no inkling of the direction, destination or destiny towards which the sailing ships would be blown by the wanton winds.

We signed our 'girmit' for that's how 'agreement' sounded to the illiterate peasants. A pidginised word with a world within it.

And 'gimityas' they became, the 'coolumbers' coolies, 10,000 miles away from the subcontinent on an archipelago of 333 islands and islets in the heart of the Pacific Ocean. It was a long, lonely journey of men and women in their youth. The exile longer than Ram and Sita's and more distant.

Children played in the village homes from where the funeral procession had gone at midday. At night, bhajans and chapters of Bhagwad Gita were recited. Or a story from the Ramayana. It's their myriad stories that must have kept them going on their bare foot in storm-tossed islands.

They lived the stories others merely narrated or acted out.

Their tales gave us some sense of life and death and the eternal cycle must continue as waves in the seas, or stars twinkling at night.

The miracle of the mortality of man is that he attends a funeral and thinks he's immortal.

The bhajans were full of such wisdom, orally transmitted over millennia and now sung on the shores of the Fiji islands, thousands of miles away from the banks of the holy Ganges.

The splendour of this transmission across vast oceans by illiterate peasants is a wonder to me today. But they sang their songs; they performed their rituals, recited mantras for thirteen days.

It seemed to me that no culture had seen death as closely as the nomadic Hindus of India. Their songs, bhajans, rituals transformed death into a living reality, an acceptance of life out of which a new life was born across mighty mountains and noble rivers.

The immortality of the soul was paramount. The body perishes; the soul moves on, wears another new pair of clothes. It was as simple as that.

Afterwards, the silence and life resumed even as we gained courage to enter the bure where the man or woman had died, where, a few hours ago, the cold corpse lay wrapped in a white cotton kaffan.

After the funeral procession had left the village on cargo lorries, a bus or two, tractors and horsebacks, we played in the courtyard where the body lay and people grieved with their intimations of their mortality as the evening descended on the hills, and a sea breeze rippled over the green canefields in the failing light of the evening sun shining in a village girl's wet hair.

Then there was darkness but you couldn't light a lamp, or cook on the earthen chulha. Food was made by your neighbours and brought to the dead person's house. Food like sorrow was shared: the burden of grief became lessened. We lived.

*

Slowly, sadly death evaporated, life resumed with food and the sounds of kava being pounded and a few men sat in the bures while women cooked in their smokey, soot-covered kitchens.

The green grass grew and we resumed work on the sugar cane plantations. In the evening, Lali had to be milked; a bundle of grass left for her to chew for the night.

Milk was in plenty, and the cow sat chewing the cud looking bovinely divine in her sad eyes, as if she knew death had taken someone who fed her by the well and gave her a wash when it was really hot.

At night, the dogs howled hauntingly around midnight.

After a few days, we walked barefoot to the little town, on the edge of the river, to see a Bollywood film full of miracles, songs, dances and a couple of comic characters.

Harry Braiya charged us a shilling to sit in the front-most seats. We thought we were given the most privileged seats until, years later, I realised these were the cheapest seats in the theatre, given to the groundlings.

But nothing diminished our enjoyment of the black and white films, and we returned home humming the tunes of some of the saddest songs of my youth. Indian filmwallahs knew how to make you weep and sing sad songs. They became part of my soul and so much of my poetry comes out of that well of sadness, the river of melancholy flow.

Yet death comes and goes; who knows why still lovely is the rose? When it happens, what does one do? It rolls through all things and you're left standing alone as cars rush by. The thing is to learn to love as deeply and intensely as you can. To visit the loved people and places where you grew up, where you'd known affections of the heart and the dreams of your mind; where your imagination is rooted in that inescapable reality that we carry till our last, living moment.

We all travel on many roads, cross many rivers and live in more than one country, one body. Fiji Indians have this particularly poignant fate. And it will continue for a generation or two. In the children, the parents will live again.

How does one cope with the grief of the soul that often seems part of the beatings of the heart? Here, a culture's great strength comes into play: while death is common, the thoughts about its acceptance have been contemplated most assiduously by the Indian mind: its epics, its mythology, its poetry, its rituals and ceremonies, its films and the daily minutiae of living with all its brutality and beauty you can experience on any city street or rustic pathar panchali in India.

Death's timelessness is what keeps many of us going. You're lying in bed looking out the window watching the birds in the trees and the wind whispering to leaves so full of green, glorious life. Next moment, you could be dead in your bed, and not a leaf from that large, wind-shaken tree will fall or mourn your passing.

To know this truth requires immense courage and acceptance of man's fate: and see life rolling through all things: to behold creation as one – one is the answer to all sums.

That answer one may find in lines of poetry which litter the lethal ordinariness of our lives, full of blessings:

> but oft, in lonely rooms, and 'mid the din
> Of towns and cities, I have owed to them
> In hours of weariness, sensations sweet,
> Felt in the blood, and felt along the heart;
> And passing even into my purer mind,
> With tranquil restoration: -feelings too
> Of unremembered pleasure: such, perhaps,
> As have no slight or trivial influence
> On that best portion of a good man's life,
> His little, nameless, unremembered, acts
> Of kindness and of love.
> … And I have felt
> A presence that disturbs me with the joy
> Of elevated thoughts; a sense sublime
> Of something far more deeply interfused,
> Whose dwelling is the light of setting suns,
> And the round ocean and the living air,
> The blue sky, and the mind of man:
> A motion and a spirit, that impels
> All thinking things, all objects of all thought,
> And rolls through all things.

Death brings to us this great awareness of Life all around us.

*

As I'm writing this, I get a note from my dear friend Rajinder in Berkeley, California. His mother, he tells me, died at the age of 107, in Hauz Kahas, New Delhi. It was from this home that I got married to Jyoti. Colonel Assa Singh and his wife became my foster-parents and their generosity was overwhelming to me; Rajinder, a couple of years younger than me, was my best friend in the college and a brilliant mathematician who later taught and researched at the University of Berkeley, California. He was from Doon School, where I spent my honeymoon year.

I visited him many years ago and have not seen him now for more than twenty-five years. But when you hear of the passing of someone who was so kind to you, how do you respond?

Perhaps by remembering their little, nameless, unremembered acts of kindness and of love.

People exist in the embers of these. And you may even see into the life and death of things. The poet knew it well and wisely, even if you do not see any more the glory and freshness of a dream.

How often I've turned to that 'Ode to Immortality':

> Though nothing can bring back that hour
> Of splendour in the grass, of glory in the flower;
> We will grieve not, rather find
> Strength in what remains behind;
> In the primal sympathy
> Which having been must ever be;
> In the soothing thoughts that spring
> Out of human suffering;
> In the faith that looks through death,
> In the years that bring the philosophic mind.

Even when your mind is high sorrowful, you find solace and comfort in the love you've known and given, which else will break your heart:

> Thanks to the human heart by which we live,
> Thanks to its tenderness, its joys, and fears,
> To me the meanest flower that blows can give
> Thoughts that do often lie too deep for tears.

And those three daffodils swaying in the breeze in my garden, so close to a blackbird's nest.

*

The great book of life and death, I think, is the Mahabharata: the Doomsday epic. The Mahabharata is too long to quote even in parts. The Bhagawad Gita, the Celestial Song, is its sublime preamble in 700 verses.

But I did read the Hindi version of this great epic, the longest in world literature, before I was introduced to English literary texts, a play of Shakespeare, a few poems of Tennyson, a novel by Charles Dickens. There's the presence of death in all these texts but they were the dying of others, far from my world on the small, distant islands of the South Seas.

The Gita contains the wisdom of ages and sages. It does contain, in my opinion, human conflict of so many kinds: you can encapsulate the world and its tragedies and trials and triumphs in its pages: its pity, its horror, its futility and its redemptive quality.

It's said it is like no other book in world civilisation.

> It includes history, legend, edification; religion and art, drama and morality. If an analogy were to be made to western culture, one would have to imagine something like the following: an Iliad, rather less tightly structured than it now is, incorporating the abbreviated version of the *Odyssey*, quite a bit of Hesiod, some adapted sequences from Herodotus, assimilated and distorted pre-Socratic fragments, Socrates by way of Plato by way of Plotinus, a fair proportion of the Gospels by way of moralizing stories, with the whole complex of 200,000 lines worked over, edited, polished, and versified in hexameters by successive waves of anonymous

church fathers. In the western tradition this seems incredible. In the Indian civilization the Mahabharata is a fact.

What is found in this epic may be elsewhere;
What is not in this epic is nowhere else.

The Gita has a wonderful image and gives a radical redefinition of death itself: just as a person changes his/her clothes, the body is discarded by the undying soul; it metamorphoses into another form or being. Demise is the word, not death. Migration to transmigration!

The soul is immortal and we do not know whence it comes and whence it goes.

For millennia, people of India have lived and borne their destiny by this marvellous concept of 'resurrection'.

In my youth, I used to hear the Gita recited and interpreted every night at the home of a dead person. It captured the essence of life and death on the eve of the great battle narrated in the Mahabharata with the epical grandeur of the warrior caste. And how often it's been repeated all over the world. Hence its extraordinary boast.

But the ordinary life of the girmityas was unimagined even in the great epic. Much of the story is about princes and kings fighting among themselves. Those battles continue even today: the elites eliminating one another. What was the Indian partition, if not an internecine war between cousins, or the European world wars, or the civil war of the USA, or the current upheavals in the Middle East and even such small places like Fiji and Bougainville? The Russian revolution or the Chinese upheavals where millions were killed: in the Mahabharata, millions are destroyed in eighteen days: with special missiles as bows and arrows.

It's all envisioned in the Mahabharata, including the treacherous as well as the sacrificing characters. The poet's imagination is godlike in its comprehension. Arjuna's vision of Krishna in supernal avatar is beyond human eyes, so Krishna first gives Arjuna the divine vision to see the viratrupam that contains everything and nothing really dies. It's a fantastic vision, oceanic in conception as if the vast oceans are nothing but reflections of the skies.

*

It now occurs to me that my girmit grandparents must have walked on the banks of the Ganges; they might have even crossed the Ganges on small boats; then they were put on sailing ships from the port of Calcutta and sailed across the seven seas to the South Seas to settle in some of the smallest islands in the largest ocean. And in their songs and bhajans, hymns, they carried this one message as travellers across the seven seas.

It's really not how many times you've crossed a river; it's really how many rivers you've crossed in a lifetime.

My parents and six siblings were born on the island of Vitilevu. I grew up on the banks of the Nadi river that watered our lives with such flourishing abundance, feeding us with fruits and vegetables in full flood. We filled our sugar sacks with floating bananas. And now my children and grandchildren are growing next to another river called by its Aboriginal name Murrumbidgee: on its banks we go for picnics.

But we often walk by Lake Burley Griffin, named after the man who designed Canberra as the national capital, a little more than a century ago. Walter Burley Griffin, a stranger to Australia, is buried in Lucknow. He died there in 1937, a city he'd gone to explore and to understand its spiritually designed multicultural circles and ethos.

Little did he know that my four grandparents had come from an antique village close to India's then most poetic city, Lucknow. Or that my grandchildren would grow in a city he'd imagined so lovingly with a lake at the heart of it and the national parliament on the edge of the lake, on Capitol Hill.

So we're connected in ways through water and land, through our suffering and salvation; and the footfalls of generations who must have walked on this ancient land with their Dreaming and songlines.

The seas connect us all. The soil gives us life. We may see our souls reflected in stars.

Life must be meaningful rather than prolonged and there are unanswerable questions of human suffering to which even the nirvana of the

Buddha couldn't find an answer, nor the crucifixion of Christ, nor the quest for moksha in the mahatma. But search we must.

The great quest continues on our endless journey of endlessness.

But they did tell us, through their own journeys and passions, that we'd be less human if we didn't understand the suffering of others. Grief is to be shared: it's part of our common humanity. It's this, above all, that makes us truly human. In death, we celebrate a life that we think is no more.

Death's natural piety binds us all like the snake coiled in Shiva's jata from where the Ganga of life-giving love flows towards the one and only ocean.

*

In my poem 'Voices in the River', I quote lines from 'The Celestial Song', translated by Edwin Arnold. I'd found a half-tattered copy in an untidy bookshop in Old Delhi's Chandni Chowk bazaar. Books in Delhi streets are as dishevelled as life or its traffic, but the roaring goes on. You get the feeling that on the ancient streets of Delhi everything coexists and the travellers walk on among sacred cows and colourful crowds and wedding bands and funeral processions. Life exists: in dung, dirt and delightful mess and distress in its dailiness. Life IS.

Lines like these are littered in my poems, here and there:

> Thou grievest where no grief should be
> For the wise in the heart
> Mourn not for those that live,
> Nor those that die.
> Nor I, nor thou, nor any of these,
> Ever was not, nor ever will not be,
> Forever and forever afterwards.
> All that doth live, lives always.
> Life is spreading life through all.

And like the ocean
Day by day receiving
Floods from all lands
Which never overflows.
Fed by the rivers
But remaining the sea always
And through all.

*

Spring is coming out in pink buds and green leaves, once again. Parrot-coloured dawns wake us up. The multicoloured parrots sit on the branches of leafless trees in the morning; some peck in the garden for worms: such mornings brighten the day and give you a sense of life, awakening beyond your life connected to other lives. And that tiny blackbird flitting furiously building its nest, digging the ground with its yellow beak, under the beautiful shimmering in the green leaves of a tree, so bare in winter, so richly laden in spring.

Children go to school on their bikes and skateboards. From my bed, through a large glass window, I behold the embracing brightness of the sun, giving us all light that IS life. THAT is LIGHT. And Jyoti breathing next to me.

And life passes as birds fly free in the sky. One never says that goodbye. Because someone you love is breathing beside you.

2. Heart's Journeys

I've been travelling for the past sixty years. For someone born in an obscure village on a small island in the largest ocean, for me this has been miraculous; someone who hadn't walked beyond six miles from the place of his birth until the age of eighteen; someone who hadn't read an English book until the age of sixteen. Someone who acquired his first pair of black shoes after passing the Senior Cambridge examination.

The beginnings of literacy and the world of books in English led me to many cities, countries, continents, universities, conferences, parliaments, writers, friends, scholars, in so many parts of the world full of natural wonders and generous humanity.

And the discovery of true love.

I entered a larger reality both of self-knowledge and joy. Now it's a world of contemplation and writing these small pieces. In my immediate family of five, almost all are readers, writers and critics. That has been a great and life-expanding gift to my family.

These pieces show parts of my travels from Nadi to New Delhi and finally arriving and living in Canberra, our home imbued with a sense of homelessness that clings to one like mud in one's childhood footsteps or tears of things: sometimes as far as the stars, always close as the eyes.

From here, I've gone to many places, met many people who have enriched my life in ways that give me joy in the last years of my wandering journeys. From here, I travel to the four corners of my world: Fiji, India, New Zealand and parts of Australia where my friends and children live. This is the country of my mind – the republic of letters, the footprints on the pages of living itself.

These are my journeys into myself.

*

That drizzled morning in June: it was 9 June – almost sixty years ago; blue haze on the ragged, mesas of Sabeto mountains – the Sleeping Giant in its lapidary slumber. I was leaving my second village, Legalega, for the tiny, tawdry Nadi airport. My natal village was Maigania, across the river, about the same distance from the airport as Legalega was from Maigania. And beyond a few volcanic hills was the larger village named Votualevu, with a primary school.

The two bigger islands in an archipelago of 333 islands and islets were named on the map as Viti Levu and Vanua Levu. I was born in a corner of Viti Levu, washed by the eternally breaking waves, blue and brilliant in the sun, wild and wonderful to behold from a mountain top. A small airport separated us from the vast ocean rippling golden in the evening sun, and touched by a perfect rainbow. We called it Arjuna's Gandiva, the weapon of total annihilation in the Mahabharat tale.

The sun did sink like lead in the sea and there was darkness – suddenly.

Maigania, Legalega and the airport formed a triangle, with the airport control tower at the apex. On the hillock next to it was the weathercock, like a giant condom, fluttering, filled with the sea breeze from the Pacific Ocean.

Legalega lay sleepily wet across the Queen's Road that wound its way by the airport to the port of Lautoka, which boasted then of the largest sugar mill in the southern hemisphere, thanks to the Indian indentured labourers like my grandparents and their children, my parents. The CSR company of Australia owned the mill and the sugar estates on native and crown lands, later subdivided into ten-acre farms for the descendants of the migrant labourers who had served their ten-year indenture in the Fiji islands. Indenture agreements had an expiry date. The illiterate peasants of India heard 'agreement' as 'girmit' – a pidginised version of a single word that defined their bondage and human bonds in so many alien lands: a word that brings 60,000 faces to my mind. And most did not return to India on a 'free passage' after serving ten years of servitude.

Many for the first time had acquired so much land, generally leased, from the native owners with the Crown Colony's sanctions: most of our Indian ancestors had been for generations peasants working on the land owned by the feudal zamindars in India. Fiji, for the first time, gave them their piece of land, albeit it was rented and owned predominantly by the native communities and the CSR company.

Fiji's first governor-general had devised a native land tenure system to prevent the alienation of communally owned lands from their original owners as was happening in Australia and New Zealand in the nineteenth century. Fiji became a Crown Colony in 1874: it's known as the Deed of Cession – a unique happening in colonial history? A few Europeans and churches had acquired large tracts of some of the best spaces on the islands.

God was good – to some. And the Fijians were not dispossessed of their land. Thank God.

Owning a piece of land for the uprooted peasants from India was a huge achievement for many oppressively caste-ridden, superstition-obsessed, ritual-performing, plundered, largely neglected communities for many millennia. They were the 'dumb millions' of Gandhi's definition, and apparitions in V.S. Naipaul's nightmare dwelling in areas of darkness like frogs in a well, covered by centuries of neglect.

But they knew their wells well. They loved India: many had grazed their sacred cows on the banks of Ganga and Yamuna. They must have surmised with their ancient instincts that rivers must lead towards an ocean. They carried in their gathries, the stories of the subcontinent. Often at night they sat and sang with simple instruments that haunt my memory with rhythms now; in the mornings, they performed their kathas and ceremonies. They went to a river or a stream or a shallow well and poured a lotah of water to the sun that rose above the volcanic mountains.

The world was charged with the grandeur of God.

They survived in their language and myths with their hard-working little communities with their petty quarrels and small ambitions. They were not sea people: they were river-dwellers. And rivers became sacred – there's no more sacred river in the world than the Ganges: Ganga Ma. Water was Gangajal.

The journeys across the black waters, kala pani, of the seven seas in human bondage also gave them a sense of freedom. It opened the world a bit more for many like a dark, dank bure with a single opening, a door of opportunity. Around them lay the utensils of another world – their mulk – which they had carried in their gathries, holdalls. The memories of mantras, myths, mud huts and the half lost languages of their village life, with songs and ceremonies never before heard in the islands of the South Seas. No cultural journey for peasant Indians was longer than this: from the obscure, moth-eaten, landlocked vegetarian villages of India to the islands among the 'noble savages' where no Indian had ever ventured. The dream of islands was a nightmare of the reality of existence.

In the islands, most living things were eaten with wild and wanton relish. This was the paradise of the South Pacific, celebrated in the adventure of literature and exploration with many far-fetched facts and peoples who rode on the saddle of Empire.

The Pacific was not part of the Indian imagination. The mythical imagination was grounded in Sri Lanka, a demonised island, in the epic the Ramayana. My grandparents were river people. They believed in gods and goddesses who lived on top of the mightiest mountains, the Himalayas, the sources of India's great rivers. I've flown over the oceanic Bharamaputra in monsoonal spate. The seas and islands were remote; the rivers and mountains were closer. They clung to their idols, made of clay, copper, wood and stones.

My four grandparents – maternal and paternal – were brought to Fiji as indentured labourers among the 60,000-plus who had begun arriving in May 1879. Many, like my grandparents, never returned to India even after their ten-year bonded labour was over: they were declared free men and women. Freedom can often be frightening to caged birds. And islands can be traps.

We were born on the island of Vitilevu, the largest in the archipelago. Our village was across the river from a Fijian koro. We hardly had much commerce or cultural communication with the native community. We yelled at each other and played in the river. Although we swam in the same waters, more than a river flowed between the two communities. Often, an older woman of the koro swam across and walked up the hill to sit with my mother and have tea. She'd bring a bunch of bananas or a couple of beautifully tree-ripe pawpaws and return home with some rice, tea leaves and sugar. But I didn't get to know any Fijian as a friend. We were kept in little cultural ghettoes. I've written about this in my books – a sprinkling of experience – but not with any intimacy or imaginative understanding.

In my school in the 1950s, I didn't have a single Fijian classmate. Christianity and Hinduism had very different religious views of life and the colonial policy of separation further deepened this divide. It was a common experience of the many scattered peoples through the colonial experience.

For all this, we had to pay a heavy price when Fiji became independent in 1970 on a communal colonial constitution. It raised its ugly hydra-head in 1987.

*

That fateful morning, 9 June 1958, I was the first in our family to make a passage back to India, the land of my girmit grandparents. My parents and all my siblings were born in Fiji on the island of Viti Levu, the largest island in the archipelago of 333 islands and islets, 10,000 miles away from their villages in the hinterland of the United Provinces. They had never seen a ship or a sea wave, although flood, famine and pestilence often ravaged their world of castes and calamities of many kinds: many died – lonely men and lonelier women – unmourned, unremembered in any epic. Yet Fiji was the most distant exile from Mother India. But it also gave them a life.

Nadi Airport was established in 1939, at the outbreak of the Second World War. Neither the airport nor the war meant much to me in my childhood spent on the banks of the Nadi river, playing soccer and gullidanda and swimming in the river from dawn to dusk with children from the Molowai koro. Our one cow Lali and a horse Charlie, two goats and two bullocks, grazed on the riparian banks of the Nandi river full of green grass and cornfields and teiteis in which dalo, kumala, yam, cassava grew in abundance among green, large leaves, under which occasionally one glimpsed human bodies wrestling, or so it seemed to my innocent eyes.

Beautiful breadfruit, pawpaws, bananas and coconuts flourished in the rich, alluvial soil. There was never a shortage of food, fruits, fish and fowls in our home. I used to love the naturally artistically designed leaves of the breadfruit tree with perfect breadfruits hidden, round, glowing like things of beauty. Below our hillock grew two mango trees loaded with Fiji mangoes. We rushed early mornings to collect the best ones unmarked by the teeth of black bats that hung on the topmost branches not unlike some latter-day preachers and politicians.

Our village world was limited, bound by a river and a feeder road that ran through the sugar fields with walls of tall green, sugar stalks sheltering us from the sun. When it rained, we huddled into the trunk of the ubiquitous rain trees, while rivulets and muddy streams ran past us into the river, which flooded with a sense of natural wildness. The flooded Nandi brought forth food and fruits aplenty. Starvation was as remote as India. And we grew with a single pair of shorts and your older sibling's shirt. Life was full of blessings; ignorance was truly blissful.

From the top of our hillock, where a tin shack stood like a sentinel with Father's booming voice, we watched the river swell, swirl and swiftly rush towards the swampy Nadi town, already under water in the rising tide.

We'd neither radio nor newspapers in the village; word of mouth was our one source of information and stark news: a shark was seen floating near Kanwa's shop in the midst of the town; some native Fijians on a bilibili carrying stolen goats had drowned under Nadi town's low, wooden bridge. At midnight their ghosts walked the one-street town. My father had caught the biggest fish in the village as it fell from the skies. A person was found dead in the mangrove, his hands held by a huge crab in the hole; apparently he'd thrust his hands in the crab-hole and the mud creature just clung to the hands; when the tide came, the greedy fellow drowned.

I believed it all as I believed that Hanumaan carried a mountain on the palm of his left hand and his devastating, menacing mace on the right shoulder as he fought the demons in Lanka, India's teardrop Serendip.

This is not as incredible as it may sound – the wind must have blown the fish from the river's surface; a shark must have come up from the sea tide that surrounded our lives with its swirling waters, hurricanes and cyclones. We, of course, didn't know the difference: knowledge comes out of experience and education both. We'd grown up on an epic where all things were possible: monkeys could fly; and demons with ten heads flourished; birds could fight in the air; bridges built by floating stones; and demons could sleep for six months at a time. And the wondrous tales of Hanuman's tail on fire could burn the golden city of Lanka.

It was all in the Ramayana. And yet Rama had scarcely taken any one from Ayodhya to fight his battles in the exiled forests or in Lanka – the loyal banar sena made a brave brigade as discovered years later in the coups.

When you live on the shores of an island, you look at the horizon, east and west, the burning rising sun, the pale sinking moon, and learn to read the weather of tomorrow in the colours in the clouds glowing against a rainbow. The waves of the sea may tell you of an impending earthquake or an incoming tsunami.

When you dwell by an airport, you often look at the skies: the vertiginous blue of the sky's infinity and the sea are reflected in the mind.

With your feet on the ground, you look up to see the planes arriving as the single searchlight flashes over the green cane fields, mountain ranges and tin huts, shaded by tamarind and rain trees. A few palms sway in the breeze like siblings after a night's strong yaqona session. A dog barks in the dark, a cock crows in a ray of light.

I'd no idea from where the PANAM planes came, deposited their rubbish, and vanished: neither history nor geography was part of my life. All you saw were white faces, ascending and descending from the aircraft. My nieghbour Nathu Mahajan carried the rubbish, collected the spoons and knives and distributed them in the village much to our delight. But we still ate with our fingers: dhal, bhaat and bhaji.

Life was all under the vast tent of blue with stars twinkling like lights of a distant city. At night, we could see strange gods and animals in the cloud formations just above the hills. Old men and women told us stories from India which they saw enacted in the clouds above. Stars shone for the air was pristine, clean.

*

As a plane landed, we ran to the airport to burn the rubbish with Mausa Nathu. He was our neighbor, a girmitya with a fair complexion. Nathu always spent evenings with Father, addressing him as zamindar – the owner of the land. India had come to us through the faces of the ageing men and women, myths and legends, tales and fables told by our grandparents. We heard her presence in songs and bhajans, in epics transformed into most incredible films which Harry Braiya showed us on white cotton sheets near a Chinese shop, full of Nepali Kashiram's pretty daughters. The Chinese had married a Nepali woman. So we went to see more than the films, which frequently spluttered in the middle and Harry Braiya sent us home only after midnight, promising another better film next week.

India was present in a million things and sounds: from utensils to multicoloured prints of gods and goddesses – each sold for a shilling, the daily wages of my indentured grandparents during the indenture. We hung these pictures on the bamboo walls. We, or at least I, prayed to our multicoloured gods and goddesses. And imagined Hanuman flying over Sabeto mountains with his mace and monkey face. With him as our guardian, we'd no fear of ghosts which, we felt, did exist in dark places, between rows of sugarcane, and across the dark waters of the Nadi river.

Then in the evening the sounds of dholak and bhajans, the film songs sung by Bisnath in his poor imitation of Rafi's voice; and occasional musical rendition of a bansoori by a cowherd from under the tamarind tree. Our world was our own – we knew little about others or other worlds.

The morning was beautiful as the sun refracted its rays in the rippling waves of the river: so much dross was turned to gold and we prayed to the rising sun.

Across the river slept a koro, full of tivoros, ghosts, we were told. And half-clad apparitions of Illmeleki and Solomoni, Blooma and Lesu.

Decades later, I saw Bimal Roy's film *Do Bigha Zamin*: two acres of land, in which the main actor is Balraj Sahni. I mention these two names because years later in Hyderabad, I met Bimal Roy's daughter, who invited me to her home for lunch and gave me a special copy of the classic film. Balraj Sahni is connected to my memory because of Bhisham Sahni, with whom I spent a week in Shimla at the IIAS. It was a delightful week with writers and scholars. I was to see Bhisham again in a moving film, *Mr and Mr Iyer*. He was a serious writer and read his enthralling work at the IIAS. *Tamas – Darkness –* is his classic work of fiction, except that it's based on the real stories of an appallingly horrible partition. Its history will continue to hurt; no monsoon rain will heal that wound.

Both Balraj and Bhisham are dead and so is dear Meenakshi Mukherjee, who had invited me to a very special conference in Shimla. Meenakshi died at an Indian airport, waiting for a flight to Delhi, I heard with shock and sadness. She'd stayed at our home in Canberra.

Together we had gone to New Zealand for a conference. At the JNU, as Professor and Head of the Department of Linguistics and Literature, she had shown Jyoti, Kavita and me the immense kindness of a friend and a scholar. She understood what the Fiji coups had done to us.

*

So we stared at the sky; and surveyed the sea to its utmost horizon, as the fireball sank behind golden clouds of a tropical sunset in the waves of the Pacific. The airport lights glimmered to welcome PANAM flights from Honolulu.

Nadi airport must have given me some subliminal wanderlust. Still in my teens, I suddenly left Nadi for New Delhi, having gone to Suva only once for my interview with Mithailal, the smartest tractor driver of the Legalega Pineapple Lines. We'd travelled together by the dilapidated Pacific Transport bus. It took around eight hours from Lautoka to Suva – a distance of 180 miles – on the winding, dusty roads, over hills and between koros, full of shouting children and squealing piglets. We arrived at the Suva bus station around five p.m. but didn't have a place to stay the night. We finally found a place called the Matanisiga Hall, recommended by a ferocious-looking taxi man with an extended moustache. He drove us there in an old Chevrolet for two shillings.

Matansiga Hall was quite something: it had dirty beds and the mosquitoes were numerous, bloodsucking. The night was a nightmare. We'd paid a shilling. We didn't sleep a wink, or forty winks.

Mithailal spent the whole night fighting the mosquitoes and telling me, Bhaiwa the mosquitoes are biting dumhdamadhumdum!

But we did survive and I attended the interview in the same clothes I'd slept in.

The panel, I remember, had several people. The Indian High Commissioner was one Mr Bhasin. One of the people present was Mr Joyce, my Natabua principal. I cannot recall any questions except one: 'What's your father?'

'He's a farmer, sir,' I had replied.

The interview was over within minutes. Mithailal and I caught the Pacific Transport bus around midday and returned to my village home at midnight.

That was my first trip to Suva but the capital had made no impression on me – all I remembered were the awful mosquitoes. Yet I was to teach there in 1966 and then life changed for me when I joined USP in 1969, after two years at SVHS in Nadi. I was first elected to the Fiji parliament in 1982.

*

The village was a small world. As we grazed our cows, from the seashore we gazed at the endless horizons illuminated by a setting sun which squirted holi colours from the copper-coloured dome. The sunsets in the Nadi seas were the most splendid I've seen: splendour falls on castle walls! The sheer beauty was breathtaking as we watched the sun go down and darkness descend suddenly on our bat-infested village with pineapple plantations with their sharp, serrated leaves like bent saws. The sun sank like a wrecked ship into the ocean as the darkness of the deep invaded our little huts.

In the morning as the sun rose over the airport above Mount Evans from Sabeto's glistening mountain range, with the Sleeping Giant protected with prehistoric black rocks like fossilised monsters, we saw our village men going to work on the plantations. One such person was Parsu, the eldest son of Nathu. He lived next to our home.

Pandit Parsu Ram, as I always addressed him, was the bhajansinger, a cynic and a sceptic. He was constantly in argument with our mutual neighbour, Birbal Pehalwaan, a surviving girmitya. Parsu was very fond of me.

His tin shed was on a hillock, beyond which was a hill with a large mango and tamarind tree, growing side by side. On the edge of the hill was a cave in which bombs were stocked for the Second World War. As we grazed our cows, we played on them, blissfully unaware of any danger. The black smoke of the war had not floated over our shores.

From his house on the hillock, Parsu could survey many houses of the village. At noon, he flashed a mirror to any woman going to the well for her midday bath. It had become his habit. I tried to portray him in a short story, 'The Judgement'. But Parsu was a complex character: he sang bhajans, holy songs; he gambled; and he was a philandering rascal. He drank methylated spirit by the bottles. He was always ready to fight with anyone who called his wife Bhauji.

In a village that was steeped in the remnants of rituals from the most prehistoric worlds of India, where mantras were chanted, ceremonies performed, stories read, the Ramayana recited, Ramlila enacted, effigies burnt; where men and women made love in between rows of sugar cane (one heard of one or two grisly murders committed with steel cane knives), we grew and went to school with our broken slates and one pair of khaki shorts, and a white, mango-stained cotton shirt, stitched by cousin Ram Autar. Semi-literate pandits and schoolmasters dominated our life of the mind. They taught us our first alphabets and numbers and made us respect the goddess of knowledge, Saraswati. To this day, my respect for the written word, in books, is supreme, sacred.

*

So on the morning of my departure from Fiji's only airport at Nadi, a huge colourful crowd had gathered to bid me farewell. I was the first person from the village leaving for India, although many had come from Indian villages unknown to us. I was going to Delhi, the capital, on a government of India scholarship. No honour could be greater, no glory more pleasing to my parents and relatives. India was the land of Rama and Krishna, Nehru and Gandhi; there were, though, a few who worshipped Hanuman and Subhash Chandra Bose. Parents had named their children after them; later after the Bollywood actors.

India and things Indian had always been important to our lives.

There were Hindi newspapers, magazines, glossy filmfares, holy utensils, songs and the quarrels of India, especially during the vivisection of the subcontinent, the communities fought but lived together. India had been part of the myths indentured Indians carried in their gathries; then those shabbily printed Hindi magazines; those pictures of Gandhi, Nehru and Bose that were pasted on our bamboo walls amidst multi-coloured gods and goddesses and black demons from Lanka. Valmiki had imagined the epical India so vividly that we were all enthralled by it and it became part of the cobwebs that webbed our lives.

The motley crowd seen at the airport that morning was never before seen in Nadi. My village folks, distant and near relatives from remote and obscure villages, many townspeople and students and teachers, had come early morning to bid me farewell. I was, it was rumoured, going to see Pandit Nehru in New Delhi on a government of India scholarship. Gandhi and Nehru were part of our songs and folklore like Ram and Laksman.

The PANAM flight had been delayed for a few hours in Honolulu. We waited. I walked in my cream nylon shirt, cotton trousers, a black coat stitched by Ratanji & Co. (London-trained, said the board in bold letters in front of his shop.) With black shoes, red socks, a red and black striped tie with a hook to hang it from the stiff collar of my shirt, I must have looked like a bridegroom from Labasa.

As the flight was delayed, I alone was invited to go into the airport dining hall for lunch. It was the first time I was seeing the inside of a dining hall of this dimension and opulence. My people all stood under tree shades outside; some sitting on the benches and looking at one gleaming aircraft on the tarmac. The steel hangar looked huge under the tropical sun. Many had entered the airport for the first time and it was quite a spectacle to behold.

The PANAM flight landed at midday. It was ready to depart for Sydney in a couple of hours. I loitered around until I was told to get ready to go. I said namaste to all my relatives and friends who had remained at the airport to bid me goodbye, much to the amusement of airport officials and customs clerks. I boarded the flight but forgot to wave that final goodbye from the last step of the gangway. I was entering another reality.

The inside of the aircraft looked spacious and huge. There were lovely air hostesses with red lips welcoming you with a smile and a drink. They taught us, first-time travellers, how to fasten our seat belts. The announcements were made in English with an American twang.

In the afternoon, the plane took off towards the ocean over tiny houses, greenfields, rain trees, swaying palms; Sabeto hills disappeared in the afternoon glare. The sea looked wrinkled like my nani's face who had come to see me and bless me, for I was going to her mulk. Her journey took weeks, months, from Calcutta to the 'Phiji' islands. But she never ever talked about it to us; and we never asked her about the world she'd left behind as a girl forever, like so many, never to return or receive a letter or a message from her parents or brothers and sisters. They were totally illiterate. My nani had the beautiful face of a rustic girl who grew up in the hills.

It was an epic exile, longer than Sita's. I was flying back to India.

*

I do not remember much about my plane trip from Nadi to Sydney. I'd no idea of city lights or a city. How we landed and went through the Australian immigration officials remains a mystery to me. At the end of the immigration corridor, one Mr Campbell found me and took me to Singh's 'Bed and Breakfast' home, run by a Fiji couple. All I remember is that I spent a cold night; at breakfast, a European lady, resplendently attired with brilliant pink lipstick, attempted to teach me how to use a fork and knife and butter my two toasts. The kindness of strangers.

In the afternoon, Mr and Mrs Singh gave me a parcel to carry for Mr Singh's brother Raj Singh, who was studying in his final year at Delhi. Soon, Mr Campbell arrived, dressed in a grey suit.

Mr Campbell must have been a travel agent – he welcomed people from Fiji on their way to India. He took me in a taxi to board the ship from Sydney to London via Bombay. It was the *Strathnaver* of the P&O. The ship was leaving Sydney for London via Melbourne, Adelaide, Fremantle and Colombo to Bombay, where I was to disembark. It was a massive boat – full of Europeans leaving for England and Europe.

The luxurious liner pulled out of the harbour in the evening – people had gathered to say goodbye to their friends and relatives leaving for 'home'. Coloured ribbons floated, shone and rippled in the slanting light of the setting sun. Around this time, Patrick White wrote his famous essay 'The Prodigal Son'. Decades later, he was to influence my life and letters. I was unaware that I'd spent a night and a day in his city when he was writing one of his great novels as I was embarking on my journey to my grandparents' country of birth.

I shared a cabin with a Gujarati business man from Sigatoka. He was on his way to Surat in Gujarat for some business dealings and to make a marriage arrangement for his son. Surat was the first British trading post on the subcontinent. It became a city of traders, grocers and migrants. We soon established that my father was a customer of his brother's shop in Nadi town. That acquaintance helped, as he was a seasoned traveller.

I was soon part of a Gujarati contingent on the ship – many from New Zealand. I didn't know there were so many Gujaratis in New Zealand. Even in Fiji we saw them only as a small business community interested in money and religious rituals. They were not even called Indians: they were 'Bombaiyas' – yet Bombay was not in Gujarat, one was to learn much later. I knew nothing about Gandhi, either. We lived in our worlds of petty prejudices.

Soon, they started cooking their own vegetarian meals, and I shared those meals rather than the variety on the ship's menu. I sat and ate with them, played table tennis with the young lively boys and girls – the girls in their shorts looked especially pretty to me. I never forgot their kindness to me and have always been fond of the Gujarati community in Fiji because of this experience on the ship despite terrible prejudice against a community that remained, as it were, behind the curtains, with their pallid women and communal clinging. They were seen mainly as a business community exploiting the indentured Indians and their descendants. That they also contributed immensely to education, economy, religion, politics, assistance to farmers and their children remains an untold story.

So Mr Chotubhai Patel and I slept in the same cabin. During the day, I played mainly table tennis and a game called 'ring' on the deck with scantily clad Aussie teenagers.

In a couple of days, I'd met two more Fiji students going to India to study. Champaklal Vithalbhai was enrolled in Delhi University in science. We became friends. The other was Bhupendra Pathik, a round-faced student, going to India to study medicine. No major incident happened to us on the ship and we journeyed on this mighty liner without fully appreciating the luxuries on board. I couldn't imagine the journey of my grandparents on sailing ships almost seven decades before. And here I was travelling in this liner back to India – the first person from my family making the return journey. I was going to Delhi, the capital of independent India without any knowledge of its ancient geography or modern history. A few films and the stories of the two epics and nani's rituals had percolated into my consciousness.

A German passenger helped me buy my first Zeiss camera. Most of my pocket money went into that purchase. But I neither drank nor smoked, so lack of money wasn't a problem, yet.

In the ship's dining hall, I'd never seen so many people at breakfast and such a variety of food on large plates; the tables loaded with spoons, forks and white napkins the like of which I'd never seen before in my life. And large, fancy menus from which to select your fare.

Our imagination was so deeply rooted in Indian mythology imported to Fiji that the mainly white passengers made hardly any impact on my mind or body. They had come from a different world and we'd nothing to do with them. The cities and ports we touched on the southern continent hardly left their impressions on my young, untrained mind and untravelled eyes.

Australian literature, history, geography, its white settlers or ancient Aboriginal people were alien to my mind. We existed entirely in our imported Indian world of villages, koros, schools, rituals and festivals with an occasional Bombay film full of mythology, melodrama, pathos, tears of mothers, bickering of mothers-in-law, sweat of poor farmers and blood of family feuds. These were familiar themes in our village lives, too, but in a much smaller world of no particular significance.

*

Days passed on the *Strathnaver* and its majestic voyage across the Indian ocean. It was only when the ship docked at Colombo that I was able to make some connections with my subliminal, subcontinental Indian sensibility.

Ceylon-Lanka had been part of us through the stories of the Ramayana and the performance of Ramlila on the village grounds. The story of Ram and Sita has had a profound grip on the Indian-Hindu psyche. The epic Ramayana has exile, abduction, war and the return of an ideal prince. The fight between Good and Evil was always emphasised when these were clearly defined. The Ramayana has been made into a holy book of the Aryan Hindus – some are still fighting battles in mythical Ayodhya, Rama's legendary birthplace, apparently desecrated by the invading Babur. Ayodhya, Jerusalem, parts of the Middle East, now Myanmar and Sinhalese Buddhists have all become ugly in the name of their god and goddess, or no godheads. The ungodly battles rage on – endlessly on the fields of human blood, the battles for God.

Personally I've never been much impressed by religious texts – most appear fake and false and full of parochial thought. Taken as literature, they have some magnificent stories and redemptive moments, but as divine revelations, in this time and age, they have limited appeal. I feel my village companion Parsu's scepticism has been more educative for me than the preaching of many priests and pastors, mullahs and maharishis.

Ceylon had come to my consciousness through the recital of the Ramayana, the most colonising text that created the native world of an island into a demon world. This perverse influence was most pervasive and persuasive to our young minds. All religious texts are essentially imperial in their civilising missions.

*

Seeing rather dark people in their boats bobbing in the waves approaching the ship was my first connection with the Indian world after the Australian shores. I was entering a different universe. I was a stranger on alien shores not unlike my grandparents in the Fijian archipelago.

But the Colombo sellers who approached the ship in their little boats had an immediate impact – I was seeing, in my mind's eye, an extension of India in their dress, colour and multitudinous presence floating on the waves. We disembarked briefly but rushed back to the safety of the ship. A kind of premonition for sights to come at our next port of call, Bombay. The bazaars began in Colombo and the buzz had not ceased in my mind as we arrived in Bombay on a bright, humid morning.

As you came down the gangplank, you were struck by the heat emanating from the pavement – it was June and the crowds of people like waves in a sea, vehicles crawling like cockroaches on the overcrowded, dirty paths, the like of which I had not seen anywhere. Coming from the New World into the Old is a journey of centuries.

Suddenly the sights and sounds of people flowing like a flooded river hit you directly in your body. And the swarming crowds everywhere you gazed. Luckily we were met by a man from the Indian Council for Cultural Relations, ICCR. He recognised three of us in the vast, madding crowd that met the arrival of the ship. Bombay was not part of my imagination. I'd not read or seen anything of this gateway to India. Pathik and Champak had their relatives waiting for them. They disappeared with them.

Here I was in Mother India's lap but with no contact, no name in around four hundred million Indians. Nor did I feel any deep feeling to touch the soil of India with my forehead as many people who visited India for the first time from Fiji did. I'd heard and read about these gestures but they were not part of my sensibility or personality.

I was taken to Grant's medical hostel, where we met two 'Fijians': Chintamani Naresh later became a friend and was studying at Ramjas college in Delhi. Anand Maharaj completed his MBBS in Bombay. Years later, my brother and his wife studied medicine there. After decades, I met Anand in Melbourne, then owner of a restaurant; he and his doctor friends in Melbourne gave us immense support during the 1987 coups. Chintamani died in Toronto and I used to get an occasional sad note from his wife about his health and state of mind. I sent him several books of mine. He was a sensitive reader and often wrote to me. He was a regular visitor to our village home in his light blue Volkswagen.

Sitting on the second floor balcony of the Grant's medical hostel, sipping sweet tea, I heard the haunting voice of a beggar woman singing a Hindi film song. I looked down: she was carrying a child wrapped in a dirty rag. To my ears, she sang the saddest song in such a way that, long after it was heard no more, her song in my heart I bore. The solitary beggar woman had penetrated my soul more deeply than anything I've seen in Bombay film to this day. It was her face in the evening sun, her voice ricocheting against the big brick houses, and the child held in her arms pleading for a few paise for a meal. I watched her disappear in the rays of the setting sun. What I had seen in a few films, I had now witnessed in real life. Something of our past had surfaced in that haunting image. That was my first real connection between Fiji and India.

In Fiji, we were poor but the word poverty was far from our minds. There was an abundance of fresh food on our farms, fish in the rivers and seas, fruits and vegetables across the river in a native teitei. My father was a visionary in education and his appetite. We always had so much food and seldom ate any 'basi' leftovers. Near our well grew fresh vegetables: tomatoes, beans, eggplants, bhindi, pumpkins, cabbages, cucumbers, okra, bhaji, watermelon, rockmelon in a two-acre patch. I watered it every morning and evening, while our cow named Lali grazed nearby and gave us huge quantities of milk out of which we churned ghee, dahi and matha. Lali was sacred to us and my mother trusted her grazing to me.

On the hillock, we had lentils of many kinds: moong, arhar, urdi, bora, peanuts; and beyond in the black soil grew sugar cane when the plantation spread to Legalega and replaced the pineapple plantations that had been the fare of schoolchildren. The pineapple factory beyond the Votualevu Junction, in two huge structures, slowly atrophied into rusted, neglected buildings.

We didn't have good sanitary facilities; near the well in the banana grove, frogs and mongoose lived. An occasional frog came out in the bucket of water we pulled from the well. I think we survived all this because of the good fresh food we lived on. Next to it was a fruitful tamarind tree and one of kathar, jackfruit. Beside it was a gorgeously leaved breadfruit tree. It produced an abundance of perfectly shaped breadfruit.

So being poor next to Nadi airport was different – a deprivation of material things. To see poverty-stricken Indians on the crowded streets of Bombay was quite another. I was entering a different level of living. It left its mark on me: perhaps that is why I plunged into politics in Fiji. But that's another story of another time.

At eight in the night, I was taken through throngs of heavily loaded porters and overfed travellers walking briskly, their heavy luggage, tin and steel trunks, carried on the turbaned-bandaged heads of coolies. The scene was incredible and no film or book could convey its living, throbbing picture. And the life that surged and swirled indescribably on the railway station, the pulsating sea of humanity on the move.

*

My experience of a train journey was from Votulevu Junction to the edge of Nadi town: the CSR had a train free for girmit passengers. It left on the railway line from Raki Raki via Tavua, Ba, Lautoka, Nadi to Sigatoka, where the journey ended at the end of the sugar farms. It took at least two days, so occasionally we got on it and arrived at Nadi town in a few hours. This was my only experience of a train journey. It was free for all, especially the girmit people and their descendants.

Then suddenly to arrive at the train station at Bombay was to arrive in a world of a river of trains, steel structures writhing and shining like pythons, a sea of people, amidst an ocean of noise, and mountains of luggage on the small heads of the red-capped coolies, some with churkis and caste marks in saffron and red powders. Every fat traveller shouted for a coolie.

I had absolutely no idea of the chaos at a major Indian railway station. Even the Bombay dock, where we disembarked from the P&O liner, had not prepared me for the Bombay railway station. I hadn't read about the railways in India: how they connected the arteries and veins of the nation with Delhi as the cobra's head with a diamond! Indian railways were the great invention of the British and slowly they became the instrument of communication and conquest. They became part of the fabulous folklore – an epic more powerful than the two marvellous ones India had produced millennia ago. The infinite distances, the teeming towns and a million villages came within the military and steel grasp of an imperial civilisation making inroads into the very old, decaying world with no protection against the onslaught of imperial conquest of the European variety.

On a train, my grandparents must have made their journey to Calcutta at the Howrah terminus. From there, they must have been herded into a depot near the port and put on sailing ships to Fiji, which many believed was in the Bay of Bengal, perhaps a day's journey away. The journey to Fiji sometimes took 100 days from Calcutta, depending on which way the wild seawinds blew.

The Bombay railway scene was one of immense cacophony and anarchy: the crowds surging, the trains arriving and departing, the whistles hooting, the porters and passengers colliding in waves, the sellers selling their wares, knowing which passengers were likely to buy their foods, drinks, and the colourful crowd moving, moving to their trains on the correct platforms like eels disappearing in the muddy darkness. Out of such chaos, great art-life, too, was created on the Indian soil.

Indian railways, I was to discover later, are ones of romance and delight unlike any other. One saw them in films but the actualities were more astonishing. Incredible India indeed with such incredible realities!

The railway station was a labyrinth – you may enter it but getting out will be a problem. There were trains puffing and groaning; there were people in their sleeping garments, and some without clothes their naked ribs rippling in the lights. At the end of the swarming multitude, you did find a train that was due to leave for Delhi. We moved from compartment to compartment – I was certain my name would not be there on the reservation lists plastered on the wall of each compartment next to the heavy steel doors.

To have arrived in India without any knowledge of the country – neither the few films I'd seen nor the epics we'd read in bits had prepared me for all this. And my grandparents, too, had no idea of this Indian experience, miles and centuries away from their obscure, unmarked villages. They did exist but existence was all in the eternal cycle of birth and death.

The vendors, the coolies, the teeming life, the noises, the sounds of unfamiliar tongues, the sights of strange dresses, the faces of people, some very beautiful, many emaciated, distressed and harassed, rushing, rushing to nowhere around at the station was beyond books, even epics. There were so many lives, an abundance of life as if in a churning ocean.

I was glad I'd found my berth and was ensconced in it, seeing only by glimpses the passengers unloading their burdens from the heads of coolies into their compartments and haggling for a few rupees of tip. And then the smell of food as they opened their boxes of greasy parathas and curries and pickles. I began to sense that, for many, a train journey was a picnic too. Indians loved eating, especially in the presence of others. And then they changed into their sleeping clothes blissfully unaware that there were others travelling with them. There was something natural in all this as it was for us to swim in the Nadi river without clothes. Nakedness was the first human condition – why feel ashamed of it?

Alone I would have never found my berth until my next birth. But the young man who was searching for my compartment and keeping a shrewd eye on me finally arrived at a steel door: on it was scribbled my name in very small letters. He read it, smiled and put me on the train. He waited with me until the huge steel monster started moving, slowly and almost noiselessly. He knew when to jump out of it and, with a final wave and a broad smile, he dissolved in the massive crowd. I was never to see him again.

I remembered his kindness as I sat not knowing where, in the gathering darkness, this train would carry me. I should have been better prepared, informed. But my village habit was inherited from my grandparents, I presume. They had got on to a train and it had taken them to Calcutta and thence in a sailing ship to 'Phiji'. My train was taking me to Delhi. But the level of ignorance was almost the same. I was lost and lonely as the train gathered speed and roared through the intensifying Indian darkness of an ancient subcontinent.

*

My companion in the berth was an army man, resplendently dressed. I was seeing an army person in full uniform so close to me for the first time. He seemed highly educated. He introduced himself as Colonel Kaul. I was too tired to talk and slept on my journey to Delhi, the moving rhythm of the train having a soporific effect on me.

The trains in India have a unique rhythm: they lull you to sleep and in the middle of the night when you wake up to go to those aluminum toilets, the rhythm sounds ceaseless and you return to your berth and sleep again. I'd no idea what landscapes we were going through. My destination was Delhi. My knowledge of history and geography was minimal – nobody taught us much about India; it was all about British history and geography. The imperial world had enveloped our minds and to think beyond those boundaries was almost blasphemous.

As the train approached Delhi's old station, you were hit by the hot breeze, as if from a suddenly opened oven. It was June, the hottest month. I was astounded to see rows of people sitting beside the railway lines, with their bare bottoms facing the train in shameless defiance, defecating. The train arrived at the Delhi station and jolted to a halt. Grabbing my grey cardboard suitcase, I got off the train to be greeted by a horde of coolies in red shirts and white safas. My eyes searched for some guide from the ICCR office, as promised, but no one was there to greet me.

I carried my bag to a black-yellow Ambassador taxi. It looked quite dilapidated but the Sikh driver put my bag on top of the car and drove me to Delhi College. The taxi stopped at the gate: inside, the building looked like ancient Moghul ruins. I left the taxi at the gate and went to see if someone could help: was my arrival expected?

No one had heard of anyone coming from Fuji.

Not Fuji but Fiji, I insisted.

'And, sar, where is that?'

Luckily, the warden of the hostel was one Mr Chatterjee. A few Malaysian students had arrived earlier. He got my suitcase from the taxi and gave me a 'room' to share with a Malaysian student named Nirmal Singh, a second-year student studying premedical. The room looked like a cave and you'd to bend down to enter it. Squirrels with their bushy tails uplifted scampered all over the place – I hadn't seen such bushy-tailed creatures before. On Nirmal Singh's head sat a colourful turban.

I had arrived in Dilli, that fabled city. One had heard of it; one had read in narratives about it; but to be in it was a dream come true. But the reality was quite different, at times nightmarish.

*

Nirmal and I became friends and he helped me survive my terrible homesickness by taking me to see films at Connaught Place, the central shopping area with elegant, modern buildings where New Delhi began. Some days we saw three pictures – Hindi and English. *The Ten Commandments* was the first picture I saw in a Delhi cinema.

We ate at Madras Café and Kake da Hotel. For a rupee, you could enjoy a most delicious meal. And we did enjoy. Food can help you survive your loneliness. We were joined by a few other foreign students, mainly from Malaysia, Mauritius, South Africa and the Caribbean, places where Indian indentured labourers were transported. Now their grandchildren had returned to study in India on 200-rupee-per-month scholarships. It was, I think, a most visionary gesture of the prime minister Pandit Nehru and Maulana Abul Kalam Azad, the first education minister of independent India.

The ICCR had organised a two-week orientation course most elegantly done by real experts in their areas. We visited many places, including the Delhi zoo, where I was seeing wild animals I'd read about in Fiji but never seen. A lion almost bit half my hand – I had pushed my hand into its cage rather stupidly. It snapped. Peacocks danced in their enclosures in their vainglory. Lectures were given on art, culture, climate, cuisine and other matters, but they had no impact on me. I was simply overwhelmed by the colours and the crowds.

All I remember of the orientation was that one afternoon a few of us were taken to meet Pandit Nehru and had tea with him. I was seated on his right – he asked me a couple of questions – Fiji was remote but not far from this most learned PM of India ever. In 1983, his prime-ministerial daughter visited Fiji and I read a poem in her presence at the Girmit Centre in Lautoka. But it's Pandit Nehru, the writer, who has touched my mind so resplendently with his words. Yet at that time I was barely aware of the greatness of the man, despite growing up with his portraits pasted on the bamboo walls of our bures. In his words there was a special splendour of thought.

After a couple of days, I visited Raj Singh, in whose brother's motel in Sydney I'd spent a couple of nights. Mr Singh and his wife had given me a parcel for Raj, a fourth-year student at the CIE in Delhi. I spent a day and a night listening to sardarji jokes.

Raj and a couple of chaps from Fiji and Mauritius had rented a flat and lived in its three rooms with three women. It was here that I had a brief glimpse of Joan, Raj's future wife. They were classmates. Later, in Fiji, we met many times and shared many meals and happy memories of our Delhi days.

When Raj retired, he and Joan settled in Gurgaon, New Delhi. Joan had by then become frail and early dementia had set in. Raj was looking after her needs with great devotion. Some years ago, I visited Gurgaon to discover that both Raj and Joan had passed on. I went to the cemetery to see their graves – their names are on it, together. Raj is described as a 'Public Servant'. But I know he was a more colourful character, known in Fiji for his stylish pipe-smoking and as an accomplished civil servant. Joan was an English teacher with Victorian virtues and attitudes. I doubt if she ever belonged to Fiji. Their talented son, Peter, now lives in Washington.

Delhi was a truly tumultuous world that flowed like the city's open nallahs in monsoon. One saw life in its abundance and in utter deprivation. The cows and the elephants, the cars and camels, the tongas and two-wheelers, the taxis, buses bellowing black smoke.

I'd come to India without reading its literature – except for the epics – and had heard a few Hindi film songs sung by my village folks in Maigania and Lega Lega. Votualevu was famous for folk-singing and Ramlila. Bombay films were sad and long, and we loved the few we could afford to see after walking six miles each way to Harry Braiya's theatre near the Nadi town's wooden bridge, the entrance to the one-street, tawdry town. Occasionally, one saw farmers in felt hats with a cane knife hung from their saddles riding their horses across the town unaware of any traffic or how their horses manured the street to the disgust of mainly Gujarati businessmen sitting on their shop verandas, gossiping in the evening shadows. They were a tribe of their own.

India was known to me through the faces and voices of the girmit people I'd seen in Fiji; many in dereliction, madness and despair. They had come from poverty-stricken places from India and Fiji didn't enrich many. They died destitute and neglected, even by their own. They had walked barefooted across shaggy hills and shallow streams to build Fiji with their bare hands and brave hearts. It was a terrible and terrifying exile for an organically close community who had lived in that old world's landscape for millennia. The islands o'er the seven seas were to be their new home for a century.

Years later, I interviewed a few decrepit old men in the Old People's Home in Samabula, and my first volume of poems *Faces in a Village* came out of it, republished in *Nadi: Memories of a River* thanks to my friend Praveen Chandra of Brisbane.

The sadnesses of these lives will haunt the Fijian landscape for generations, not because there wasn't slavery or indenture before then but because most of the people thus transported today have a country and a home. The girmit people have often felt homeless in their homes. The fate of their children is another story of profound displacement.

In Fiji, it was not only the land that was denied but a permanent citizenship. Indigenous racism of a few led to three brutal coups in the past thirty years against the descendants of a defenceless people. This is the unique predicament of a postcolonial inheritance. It's only now, since 2013, that an equality of common name has been granted in the new citizenship, a constitution. If it lasts, it will redeem more than an Empire's grave injustice.

I hadn't read any writers on India. Rudyard Kipling, E.M. Forster were totally unknown to me. No Indian writer featured in our imagination. I knew little about identity or living in an alien and alienating landscape. Much of this sense of place, of being, of belonging, is deepened by losses and an awareness of an inner emptiness. I, in my ignorance and innocence, was blissfully uneducated, with an undeveloped heart.

Initially, Delhi was a place of deepening disillusionment. I found it difficult to cope with the daily preoccupations of life. A sense of anguished loneliness permeated into my spirit like some virus that remains glued forever in the inner entrails of your life.

Delhi College now is Zakir Hussein College. I was there for three months but had to travel to the uni campus in Old Delhi – our classes were held in the university. I'd to take DTU Bus 21 every morning and it became an impossible journey – the buses were overcrowded. I couldn't get on one. My misery was compounded. I was desperate – this was not my world at all. I was alone in the swarming tide of Indians. I was drowning; Indians were waving – from the smoke-belching buses – and people clung to them like barnacles.

*

One evening, in utter desperation, rummaging through my cardboard suitcase bought from the shop of Kanwa Patel in Nadi town, I came upon a note given to me by the then principal of Jasper Williams High school in Lautoka, Miss Majorie Hodge. The envelope was addressed to 'Shri Bernasidas Chatuvedi, Rajya Sabha'. I'd forgotten all about it.

Miss Hodge had given it to me one afternoon when I went to visit Kaka Jaddu's only daughter, Sheilawati, a form four student at Jasper. She was my smartest cousin and at that time the most educated woman in my entire extended family. I had gone to say goodbye to her. You couldn't, of course, meet a girl of the school without going first through the principal's office.

When Miss Hodge heard from the clerk that I was going to India to study on a scholarship, she came out of her office, shook my hand warmly in a large, Australian grasp. She was a big woman. She made me sit in her office, and wrote a note and gave it to me. I slipped it in the front pocket of my nylon shirt without realising the significance of Miss Hodge or Shri Chaturvedi, to whom the note was addressed.

Now suddenly in Delhi, I found the envelope. That day, I didn't go to the university – instead, I took a bus to the South Block in New

Delhi where I'd the vague idea the Rajya Sabha was located. I finally found the quarters where the Rajya Sabha MPs resided. I knocked on the small white concrete wall of a house. A chaprasi opened it, dressed in khaki clothes. I handed him the envelope. He examined it thoroughly and then took me into the inner courtyard. He went in. Soon, he came out and invited me into an open space covered with green grass.

On a morah sat a bent figure with books and papers spread around him. He offered me a glass of nimbupani. Hon. Benarsidas Chaturvedi had read the note from Miss Hodge and asked, 'Can I help you in any way?'

I asked him if he could assist me to change my college from Delhi to Hindu on the campus where a couple of my Fiji friends studied, especially Champak Vithalbhai, who had travelled with me from Sydney to Bombay on the *Strathnaver*. Shri Chaturvedi scribbled a note to the vice-chancellor, Dr V.K.R.V. Rao, a formidable economist. I left him with a bowed namaste, as he sat bent, writing.

It was only after many years that I realised what a remarkable man and journalist Benarsidas Chaturvedi was. In Fiji, I'd never heard of him. That he'd devoted much of his life fighting for India's freedom and freeing indentured Indians especially of Fiji, I'd no acquaintance with. It's only when years later I read K.L Gillion's pioneering work *Fiji's Indian Migrant*s that I discovered it was dedicated to 'For Benarsidas Chaturvedi'. Ken Gillion was a New Zealander and his book was a gift to us. Benarsidas was a distinguished Hindi journalist who had ghost-written Totaram Sanadhya's girmit experience in *Fiji: The Story of the Haunted Line* and *My Twenty-one Years in Fiji*: two classic and unique documents narrated by an indentured labourer.

Most indentured labourers were illiterate : they were born, grew up practising rituals, singing bhajans, procreated and died – unmourned, unwritten, unremembered. But not quite forgotten thanks to the richness of their oral traditions. And their immutable connections with their India.

Totaram's texts affected Gandhi and his disciples, among them C.F. Andrews, and finally led to the abolition of the abominable indenture system. But the books were unknown to people of my generation. If they are known now, it's only to a select few. This is the tragedy of not only a colonial education but a community's indifference to its own history and lack of curiosity. History is unimportant to a people hidden in the hinges of history, still handcuffed.

To make up for this neglect, during the Girmit centenary celebrations in 1989, as a member of the Fiji Girmit Council, I suggested we invite Shri Chaturvedi as the chief guest at the centenary celebrations in Fiji. The idea was warmly supported, but by then it was too late as old age prevented him from taking long flights to a distant archipelago about which he had written so much and agitated so compellingly against the humiliation of the girmityas in the South Pacific.

In the 1990s, I was a guest at the Cumberland Lodge situated in the Great Windsor Park. My friend and fellow traveller, Dr Alastair Niven, was the then principal of the Lodge. I stayed there for a few days among the most beautiful oaks towering like cathedrals. Ben Okri and I were at a Sunday service and presented to Her Majesty after a solemn service in the ancient royal chapel. But what I found most valuable was that the librarian, when she discovered I was from Fiji, gave me a book as a gift: *Charles Freer Andrews* by Benarsidas Chaturvedi and Marjorie Sykes, with a foreword by M.K. Gandhi, published in 1949. I've treasured that book with three of the noblest names associated with the girmit experience of Fiji. Recently, it was the centenary of the abolition of this one hundred years of servitude – another human stain on our humanity.

*

With the handwritten note from Shri Benarsidas, I walked into the large rose garden of Dr V.K.R.V. Rao's residence. He was having an evening party of some sort but his peon gave him my note. He called me into his office, made me sit on a maroon sofa and scribbled a note to the principal of Hindu College, Mr Raj Narain Mathur. The note had a single line: 'Please see what you can do for this scholar from Fiji.'

With the note firmly clutched in my right hand, I ran to the Hindu College principal's office. There I waited, as the chaprasi wouldn't let me enter the office.

Finally at five p.m. I was allowed to see one Mr Mahabir, apparently the clerk to the principal. Any office of some importance had its own hierarchy, I was to learn later: the chaprasi took the note from you; he passed it to the peon, who handed it to the clerk and then got him a cup of tea.

While Mr Mahabir scrutinised the letter from every angle, you waited expectantly. Then Mahabir looked up at you; you bowed with a namaste and a smile. Then he handed the note to the principal's personal assistant, Mr Bhatia.

Mr Bhatia read it at least twice and then called me in. 'So you've come from Fuji.'

'No, sir, Fiji.'

'And where's that?'

'Beyond Australia, sir.'

'Ah, Austria? Hitler was born there.'

'No, Australia.'

'Ah, Mr Bradman's country?'

Now I hadn't heard of Bradman, the great cricket legend. I knew nothing about cricket or the boy from Bowral. I took the risk and nodded, politely.

'Wait here, Mr Satendra.'

I did.

Mr Bhatia went into the principal's office. He emerged after five minutes with the note, on which was scrawled, 'Admit this scholar.'

I was admitted on a brown, frayed form.

I was delighted and went to see my Fiji friend Champaklal Vithalbhai from Suva. Champak took me to the university café for a cup of tea and samosas.

A day had changed my destination and destiny, as days often do. My Fijian peasant boldness had paid off.

*

That weekend, I brought my meagre belongings to the college hostel. I was happy and the room was much better than the one at Delhi college. Around 7 p.m, I went to dinner with Champaklal, who was looking around him nervously. Before I could put a morsel of chapatti and half-cooked rajma dhal in my mouth, a voice shouted, 'Feejee!'

I looked up and there was a fair-looking fellow standing tall between Champak and me.

'Come with me, you rascal!' he ordered.

I protested meekly, 'Let me finish my meal.'

The chap, half-shaven, with bloodshot eyes, dishevelled hair, half-dressed, cut a rather wild figure. He roared, 'Sale, bahen…come now!' Expletives flowed from his ugly mouth like lava from an erupting volcano.

I had never heard such hideous language, and stood petrified.

Champak jumped from the table and vanished. I was suddenly surrounded by three other well-fed 'dogs', barking at me with a ferocity I'd never encountered. They dragged me to the courtyard. In the middle was a slab of concrete. I was made to take off my pants.

'Take off your panties, sale,' shouted a rather large Punjabi man.

I obeyed.

'Now sale, bahen. Do what we tell you. Show us your crown jewels.

'Crown jewels? They're with the Queen of England,' I managed to utter.

They laughed uproariously.

'Sale, show us YOUR Kohinoor, bahen…,

'Arre, sale, show that Fijian thingmejig!' One fair finger pointed at my penis.

They examined it with their dirty hands. Then the tallest one, with reddest eyes, put a rupee coin on the concrete slab. He directed me to push it to the other end.

As soon as I extended my forefinger to touch the coin, one of the bastards barked, 'Not with your finger, you rascal. Use your tool.'

'I've no tool,' I protested, half weeping.

'Are sale, that tool.' He touched me with his forefinger.

I'd to push the coin from one end of the slab to the other with my Fijian organ. It did the job.

There was clapping and laughing. I was weeping.

Then one chap by the name Bulbul came forward and shook my hand and asked me to dress up. 'We'll take you to the canteen.'

There they ordered coffee, samosas and cutlets. We ate and drank coffee from clay pots. At the end, I was asked to pay the bill. I did.

'From tonight, we're your friends,' said Bulbul. 'Don't let anyone bully you, okay?'

I was too miserable to say anything, and disappeared in the summer night of Delhi into my room, wondering why I'd come to this college full of ruffians. The light in my room had fused, so I lay on my bed, on the mattress sold by Mr Khanna, stared at the peeling ceiling full of insects. And a lizard slithering, gulping moths with its lightning tongue.

As the long summer twilight perished, a deep sleep embraced me.

*

The ragging in the hostel had come to an end. I joined the English Hons class at Hindu College and made several friends.

One of my dearest and long-lasting friends has been Kunju Bala Subramaniam from Malaysia. We're still in touch and see each other at least once a year – he lives in Malaysia and runs a big medical clinic with his son, Rajah. Kunju has been a generous friend.

There was only one girl in the Hons class, named Tapti Biswas. She was always smiling at me – perhaps with some sympathy for a foreigner.

Years later, I was to read V.S. Naipaul's *A House for Mr Biswas*, one of the classics of modern literature. Tapti was a Bengali and I suspect Vidia Naipaul had a Bengali ancestor. Decades later, I discovered two of my dear Bengali friends in Debjani and Rana Ganguly.

Several dadas, the raggers, were from the senior English Hons class. People like K.C. Mehra, an actor and a bit of an activist; and Akashlal, a cricketer. I began doing well in my class, which meant that I was writing THEIR essays for them for second and third years. It did help me to become the manager of the hostel mess. I took the position seriously and the warden appreciated my ability to keep the hostel food to a certain standard. The food contractor gave us the best meals on a separate high table. We relished the petty power; while others ragged the new arrivals into the hostel.

One night, I was called by the warden in great alarm. We rushed out in front of the hostel and there were two gangs with knives and iron rods, cursing one another in the variegated vulgarity of their mother tongues. A terrible fight was brewing and my hostel mates watched from the balcony of the first floor for the impending excitement of a bloody encounter.

That night, my innocence, call it ignorance or naivety, saved the day. Unaware of any danger, I went and stood between the two warring factions. The cause was ragging – a goonda was brutally ragged by Bulbul and his colleagues. The goonda had got his gang and wanted his revenge. For some reason, this ferocious-looking man listened to me and the bloody confrontation was averted. From that day, I was called the prince of peace. The warden gave me a bigger room next to his.

No major mishap happened in the first two years but during the third and final year at the college, we became quite friendly with some of the senior Hons students at St Stephens. They began liking me and invited me to their special dinners after I'd won the Best Director's Prize in the annual drama competition organised by Rupin Walter Desai, our favourite lecturer and a lover of Will Shakespeare.

*

When the new students arrived, ragging began again – we were now the dadas. One night on the main road, between our colleges, young boys were made to stand naked and wave at cars – in fact, salute the passing vehicles, shaking their tools. This went on for two nights; on the third night the students were made to stand in the middle of the road and stop the cars.

A particular car was stopped – there were three giggling girls in it and a man in suit was sitting in the front seat. The ragged boys saluted the old gentleman, smiled at the teenage girls and then let it disappear into the dark night.

Suddenly two police cars, their sirens in full blast, arrived from the two sides. The naked boys were bundled and taken to the station; we were safe behind our college gates. The boys were released only after midnight. Much to our chagrin, we discovered that the car had belonged to a high court judge and he was outraged and reported the vulgarity of the students to the police.

After this incident, ragging stopped between our two colleges. And life became normal. We concentrated on producing *Julius Caesar* for our college's main annual cultural event. We got quite close to Rupin Desai and used to visit Chandni Chowk, the old bazaar in Old Delhi, near the Red Fort, for appropriate costumes and swords and staves for the mob in *Julius Caesar*. It was there that I discovered what treasures lay in that overcrowded bazaar full of people, cows and cow dung.

Suddenly, one saw an elephant or a camel in the cacophony of life. We had parathas in abundance with ganne ka juice and nimboopani – in dirty glasses. But they were delicious and I think we must have developed deep immunity to many diseases.

Years later, with my children, Jyoti and my brother-in-law Anup Kumar Seth from St Stephens, we visited Chandni Chowk and had thirty-two varieties of parathas in the prathawaligali in a shop where the owner proudly showed us that the shop was started in the 1880s and among the visitors who relished the parathas made by his grandfather was Pandit Nehru. To confirm it, he brought out a couple of faded newspaper photographs with Pandit Nehru and his companions in the shop.

This was Old Delhi. It must have known its glory days – the Red Fort, the Jama Masjid, one of the world's greatest mosques, the temples and gurdwaras – all coexisting in that space that was old India with colourful crowds of people in an ancient world. It was the largest bazaar I'd seen.

*

Not far from it was Daryaganj, one of my closest friends' home. Deepak Seth's home was upstairs in an old building. Deepak's father was a printer and publisher, mainly of Hindi books and magazines. I spent a lot of time at his place and years later it was Deepak who published my first book of poems, *Faces in a Village*, in 1975; and subsequently, *Lines Across Black Waters* in 1997.

Deepak was to take over the business from his father and won a couple of major awards for excellence in printing and publishing. Deepak's younger brother became a doctor. Deepak married Leena and they have two children. He's one friend from my college days with whom I'm in touch even now – we meet in Delhi whenever I pass through the most teeming modern-ancient city I've lived in and known.

I was a good student in my Hons class – although the most knowledgeable person was my dear late friend Ramesh Rao, perhaps the most well-read. His father was a professor of psychology in the university. His comments on the texts were most incisive and learned. We all centred around him and visited his home in Shakti Nagar for South Indian meals virtually every Sunday and copy his notes for our assignments.

Ramesh married later; I heard in Fiji that he was almost burnt to death when his wife self-immolated by pouring petrol on herself. Ramesh was saved. Later he went to Canada. I met him in the 1990s in New Delhi. He was still the same witty friend but one of the burnt ones. When I returned to Fiji from Delhi, I heard Ramesh had died of cancer. He was the first close friend of my youth who had gone.

Now when I meet some of my friends in Delhi, we talk about him and his immaculately written essays. Some of his classmates copied his essays to pass their exams. Ramesh himself wrote slowly – a handicap for writing examination in eight papers.

Of the Class of '61 two of us got Div 2, the rest were all Div 3, including Ramesh. In the whole university there was only one Div 1 that year. When we went to check the results posted near the registrar's office, we looked first at the Div 3. My name was not there. I was in utter despair, about to wail at my failure, when Deepak said, ' Look up, sale!'

My name was at the top of Div 2. From fail to be transported to that height was joy enough. We celebrated despite my friends' incredulity that I had scored a second while the rest were in third! But in my heart I knew Ramesh deserved a FIRST.

At Hindu we'd a drama competition – either a one-act play or a scene from Shakespeare. A number of performances were entered for the competition – I, too, became a director. Having done *Julius Caesar* for the Senior Cambridge examination, I directed the 'quarrel scene' towards the end of the play when the two conspirators go to their doom. On the eve of the battle, Brutus and Cassius quarrel with each other. I'd always found this scene quite poignant and its deep psychology remains part of my psyche.

Brutus was a friend from the Economics Department, Dev Kumar Ghatak; Cassius was my friend Sudhir Chandra Agarwal. Both agreed to play their role with acting elegance and passion. I was awarded the Best Director's prize. This gave me an overnight fame. But more significantly, our favourite lecturer Rupin Walter Desai liked the scene so much that he made me the secretary of the Globe Society. Desai produced a Shakespearean play every year – the highlight of our college's cultural life.

In the third year, we produced *Julius Caesar* to great acclaim and appreciation. For much of the first half of year, we didn't study but concentrated on the production. During the production of the play we discovered a remarkable friend in Rupin Desai. After more than fifty years, we're in correspondence and whenever I'm in Delhi we meet him for dinner or lunch at his home, Rangoonvilla. Desai's love for Shakespeare remains unabated and legendary. *Hamlet Studies* – scholarly writings on a single play – has been going on for decades under the editorship of R.W. Desai, one of the world's most eminent Shakespearean scholars.

During the rehearsals, a first year student joined the department. She would come and watch the rehearsals sitting at the back of the hall. Most of us were busy with the play in the front but D had his own play going at the back. He was infatuated with Kusumlata, alias Dynamite.

I was given the task of revealing D's Romeo-like passion to Dynamite. You've to understand that for many of us girls were forbidden fruits. D was in my category without any knowledge of how to approach girls or suggest a date. So one fine day to impress this girl, D dressed up, and I travelled in the same bus. D sat opposite Dynamite and I sat at the back: my task was to show when D's smile was at its best by raising my finger – one meant okay, two was very good, three was excellent – and he had to maintain that smile. Alas, Dynamite paid scant attention to D smiling tenderly, in his best red pullover. The experiment to lure the lady was a distinct failure.

Next day, we'd a conference over coffee, cutlets and hot samosas. D paid for it all. Ramesh was indifferent to this drama with his favourite expletive, 'sale bahen'! Ramesh was from the south, a Tamilian, so Hindi expletives had quite a twang when he rolled them down his tongue and spat them out like hot chillies mingled in rasam.

Chander Prakash, another friend, suggested, 'Give the silly girl a cold shoulder for a while.' How dare she be indifferent to D's best smiles in his best pullover and an expensive pair of blue jeans.

However, D asked me to go and talk to her and tell her about his burning passion. Like a fool, I accepted this suggestion and met Dynamite, who listened to my pleadings on behalf of my friend. But to no avail – my mission was as silly as it was a failure, something akin to a scene in *Pride and Prejudice*.

Then we followed Chander's suggestion. We thought this a bright idea until one day we discovered that Chander Prakash, our friend, was buying and giving her quality chocolates. It led to a quarrel between two friends. As it happened, Dynamite already had a boyfriend who used to come on a roaring motorbike and take her to Connaught Place for cinema in the evening.

We lost interest in Dynamite, who in her own way had exploded several macho myths of my spoilt friends. Meanwhile, Sudhir had fallen in love with Gul K, giving her wild rides on his old scooter. The confessions of his heartaches deepened our friendship and we became close friends. I was always a sympathetic listener, never having had a girlfriend myself. As I'm writing this, Deepak – now in his eighties and just returned from Boston, where his son Kabir now lives – wrote to me that Chander Prakash is in Montreal, dying of cancer. Deepak couldn't visit him because it was so difficult to get a visa to Canada from the USA. He was asked to apply from Delhi.

Another friend I made was Pradeep Maitra – he was senior to me and a lover of Shelley's poetry. We spent a summer together in the hostel. Pradeep later joined St Stephen's College for Masters and he used to invite me to dinners there – a special ritual every week in the dining hall of the college and a much more elegant affair than in the Hindu hostel.

The three years at Hindu were happy ones. Ramesh, Chander, Deepak, Sudhir, a quartet – we were inseparable. Later, Rajinder P. Singh joined our group but everyone treated him affectionately like a baccha – a Doon School kid.

Rajinder became my very close friend. He came from a rich sardarji home – his father was a retired medical colonel in the Indian army. His elder brother Peter was a MIG pilot. His sister Jasbir was about to get married to an army officer. Rajinder had a younger brother also but he was in some boys' hostel and I hardly ever saw him in Delhi.

Rajinder's mum and dad lived in their very elegant home in Hauz Khas. At weekends, I used to ride with Rajinder on his green-hued Bajaj scooter to spend a night or two at his home. The food was the best and the Sikhs ate well. Rajinder's mum was fond of making gulab jamuns, a sweetmeat I relished in abundance.

Their home became my home and when I got married, my baraat went from their home to the wedding hall in Colonel Assa Singh's chocolate-coloured Chevrolet. The generosity of the Sikh family has remained in my heart and often I remembered the few old Sikhs we'd known in Votualevu and Nasau. They were wonderful farmers and in my life I've never seen a Sikh beggar: an extraordinary community of India. They were always a brave and hard-working people in my experience. It was only when Indira Gandhi was assassinated by her two Sikh bodyguards that the innocent Sikhs suffered greatly in parts of Delhi – heinous acts of political revenge so common among the subcontinent's several partitioned communities.

My friends were part of the English Department. We were supposed to be the smartest group in the college. English still dominated, although the Englishmen and memsahibs had gone after 200 years of haughty rule. What an Empire they had created: it's said in sheer absent-mindedness. But the love-hate relationship of this unique imperial adventure lasted long after the empire was reduced to rubble, a pool of mud. The real glory now lay in its pollination and cross-fertilisation of ideas in the minds of Indians. This was most deeply reflected in the departments of English, the chosen tongue, and in the many institutions and the national idea of India itself. India's first prime minister had, after all, studied at Harrow, Cambridge and the LSE. Parliamentary democracy and many ideas of freedom had entered the inner Indian landscape through a hundred years of struggle through servitude, within and from outside.

Across the road was St Stephens College, where C.F. Andrews had been a lecturer, before he became a disciple of Gandhi. The lawns of the Christian college were well-manicured and the malis kept the garden fresh and green like the saris that some of the girls from Miranda House wore. The campus was a most enjoyable place in Old Delhi. On the jungle ridge, peacocks danced when it rained. There were huge black rocks and we'd go and sit on them to see the dance of the peacocks. I must say such sights bewitched me. On the wide main road, we were surrounded by monkeys, and if you teased them, they would follow you to the gates of your hostel. There were cows grazing on the college campus to give us milk in the morning. Space was plentiful – while Delhi College was squeezed between a bazaar and a red-light district, Hindu had the space for many gods and goddesses.

The almost three years at Hindu College turned out to be delightful and productive. I was glad I hadn't returned to Fiji – the first few weeks in the Delhi summer, in the loneliness of the swarming crowds, had been too much for me. Luckily, my father didn't have the money to buy my return airfare. I doubt if anyone more ignorant or innocent ever travelled this far in the second half of the twentieth century.

The two summers spent in the hostel were most pleasant and I read widely. One summer, my companion was a Buddhist monk from Cambodia. I don't remember his name, but for reasons I cannot fathom, he was very kind to me. With him, I got to know a community of Buddhists whose abode, monastery-like, I visited on many weekends for lunch, the most delicious I've eaten.

On weekdays, in the evenings, my monk friend walked to Kamla Nagar to learn typing. I used to accompany him: while he spent his time in a typing school, I browsed through many books at the International Bookshop run by a sardarji, elegantly turbaned. I began buying books on credit. I wish I had learnt typing with my friend. For years, this lack has been a costly handicap for me as a scholar and a writer. Only recently have I begun word-processing my own writing with my right forefinger.

The International Bookshop had books from the US and the UK. The owner gave me books on credit to be paid at the end of the month when I received my stipend. I spent most of my money on buying books and eating tutti-frutti ice cream in the evenings.

My favourite restaurant was Eat More, run by a Pathan. From the outside, it looked rather unappetizing but the food they served – naans, parathas, tandoori rotis, meat curry, dhal were the most delicious. I wasn't aware of the variety of Indian cuisine – Fiji cooking was my favourite. We'd no fridge and most goats, fowls, fruits, vegies, grew on our farms. The manager Pathan took a special liking to me and my friends. Sometimes, we'd a meal for a rupee – two chapattis and a meat curry. How we relished every morsel when money was short!

Fifty years later, a Pathan student came to study in Canberra – he joined my university and I took special care of him until he completed his doctoral studies and became a lecturer. Recently, he came back to Canberra to live while his wife is a professor in medicine at the ANU. I wonder if I would have taken him under my wings if that unknown Pathan, the manager of Eat More, hadn't been so kind to me in my impecunious days at Delhi University.

Dr Adeel Khan died in Istanbul two years ago, alone in a hotel.

Next summer, I was joined in my book-buying obsession by Pradeep Maitra in his final Hons English class. Pradeep had a love for books and tweed coats. He also loved fish curry – a Bengali delicacy, I learned later. We became dear friends and spent the summer in the hostel. We cooked our lunch, mainly fish and rice, and read our books. He loved the poetry of Tagore and Shelley; I liked Wordsworth's poetry and the novels of Thomas Hardy.

We also began eating dinner at a more upmarket restaurant named the Prince; again, the owner began giving us meals on credit. He was a big-bearded sardarji with a bigger heart. We paid him at the end of the month when I got my stipend, amost like my father used to pay his annual credit to the shop of Tikambhai, when he got some money from the CSR company. Tikambhai wrote in his Gujarati hand whatever he wanted. And then one fine day he died. His son Shannu, my primary schoolmate, couldn't run the shop and I think he closed it because few farmers were willing to pay their debts to the son they owed to the father. Shannu used to visit my sardar brother and ask him to help collect the debts from the many village homes. My brother assisted him, I suspect, because Shannu didn't ask him to pay his debt.

Together Pradeep and I bought books. Book-buying has remained with me just like the habit of living on credit. I've never been able to resist the temptation of buying a book I wish to read or have read about. Or one for Jyoti or my children. Or for a dear friend. I must own my copy. Now of course, Jyoti, Gitanjali and Kavita are deep literary readers. And our granddaughter Hannah Maya seems to have inherited the habit.

A book is the best gift I often receive from friends and family. And give to others, including my own!

*

At Hindu College, we'd a single room with bare white walls, a rough hewn table and a chair, and a charpai-like bed. We'd to buy our own sheets, a mattress, blankets, a reading lamp, and a pillow. And a whirring fan that revolved like a wounded bird; if you accidentally touched it, you felt it could electrocute you instantly.

Somehow Mr K.K. Khanna of Kashmiri Gate always surreptitiously obtained information about the arrivals of foreign students in the college hostels. Around ten a.m. sharp, Khanna knocked on the door. He was a Punjabi businessman, I now realise – that is, a man from the tragically partitioned Punjab state. In my mind, every Punjabi was a turbaned Sikh, a knowledge I'd acquired in Fiji. Just as every Gujarati was a fair, paltry business man and his wife a pallid woman wrapped in a cotton sari. It took me years to understand that both Gujarat and Punjab are peopled with a variety of people of many colours, physiques and occupations. I've now visited both states from Patan to Chandigarh – the hospitality has been overwhelming and my knowledge has deepened.

Mr Khanna was an amiable sort of fellow, the like of whom I hadn't encountered in Fiji. In fact, he was a salesman of considerable charm, with a pockmarked wheatish complexion, paan-stained teeth, dyed black hair. He had rather large hands and was around two metres tall. He dressed in the latest stitched shirt and trousers, with white shoes. It took me years to realise he was imitating some Bombay film actors.

Khanna would come and sit on your spartan bed, pressing the mattress rather hard and then looking at you with deep sympathy – his eyes suggesting how could you sleep on this bed with such meagre beddings? Personally, I'd no problem – all my life in Fiji, until the age of eighteen, I slept on a bamboo plass with dry grass sewn in gunny bags as our mattress. We covered ourselves with a paal or a torn black blanket.

Khanna would chat with you as if he had been waiting for you for days. After the usual questions: 'Satendraji, arre, accha, when did you arrive from Fuji?'

'Fiji.

'Arre haan Fijistan, where is it?'

The map made by Moti publishers and sold by Atma Ram and Sons didn't show it. So you pointed to two dots in the vast Pacific. In fact, you pointed to New Zealand.

Mr Khanna was least interested in geography. 'Wery far, wery, wery far? Indians live there too? Big, big place?'

You could sense he was in a hurry to visit several students, new arrivals, in the hostel. And by the time he left, he'd have convinced you that you needed to buy several things for your bed and room from his shop, the latest arrivals. 'Don't worry about the money – you can pay me every month. You are not running away.'

Some did, without paying.

Khanna became my friend. He thought I was a good student, unlike many foreigners only interested in girls. One day over a cup of tea, he confessed to me that he was in love with a rather tall Fiji girl. I didn't know the girl at all – she was studying at Miranda House, Delhi's most modern college for women. Khanna wanted me to introduce him to Ms Fiji, as he called her.

I approached Raj. He was well-versed in affairs of women. He was completing his BEd at the CIE, the premier teacher training institute in India. He and his two flatmates had their own girlfriends. Raj advised me not to take Khanna near her.

It was Raj who told me that Mr Khanna was a crooked fellow. Besides, the Fiji girl had a boyfriend, a minor prince who lived in the room next to mine. His name was S.S. Singh and we became friends. Sometimes in the middle of the night, he'd come and tell me of his escapades. I listened to him with deepest interest; then he'd leave my room after borrowing a few rupees and an underwear.

Surinder's romance came to a sudden end. Ms Fiji got engaged. Years later, I met her once in a city: the lovely girl from Fiji had shrivelled but she lived in a big house surrounded by flowers, married to a plump banker. She smiled a lot but the sadness of a lost love haunted her face evermore:

> *Ankho mein nami, hansi labon par*
> *Kya hal hai, kya dikha rahe ho*
> *Kya gum hai jisko chupa rahe ho*
> *Tum itna jo muskura rahe ho...*

*

One summer, a friend named D.D. Joshi and I borrowed some money, sold my camera, and went to Shimla, the summer capital of the Raj. We stayed there for three weeks at the YMCA. The manager was a decent man – he accommodated us in a large room reserved for special guests. It was there that I met several Mauritian students who became my friends. Most were doing their courses in Medicine. But they had come to Shimla because a lady with Mauritian connections was the health minister in the state government. Joshi and I used to cycle to their spacious government bungalow and have lunch. She'd a daughter about our age, so she was an added attraction to several Mauritians.

We spent the afternoon playing cards. I also befriended a man from Ethiopia who was generous beyond words and took Joshi and me to the most expensive restaurants for meals. We enjoyed his rich hospitality.

One of the great losses of life is to lose touch with your college friends. I did, with many, especially with D.D. Joshi and Pradeep Maitra. I never saw them after I left Hindu College.

But Shimla remains in my mind – the only hill station I visited during my college days. Today Shimla is the capital of Himachal Pradesh. Jyoti and I were there at the Indian Institute of Advanced Study for a few days in July 2015. Jyoti gave a paper at the university; I gave a seminar at the IIAS. Both of us were invited to spend some weeks in Shimla. We'd a wonderful time and if I were younger, I would have gone there again for a longer period.

I met one of my Mauritian friends in the 1990s as the Mauritian High Commissioner to Canberra – Dr Gyan Nath became a dear and generous friend and supported Fiji's return to democracy during the aftermath of the first two coups. He was at heart very much the girmityas' grandchild. But of course we'd no idea how much in common we'd with Mauritius, Trinidad, Guyana and even South Africa. It's only when I began reading the writings of these girmit descendants that I began to see a distant pattern in our shared history. But that history with a human face and fate is yet to be written.

I've written of my second journey to Shimla to attend an Indian ACLALS conference in the 1990s. It was organised by my three friends Meenakshi Mukherjee, Harish Trivedi and Santosh Sareen. That delightful trip is published in my book of journeys, *Beyond Paradise: Rights of Passage*. Sadly, Meenkashi is no more. And I remembered her with great feeling when Jyoti and I went to the IIAS in July. We were returning from our rather long trip from Göttingen in Germany. During that ACLALS, I met Debjani, who became a dear friend and later came to Canberra to study and work. She and Rana are now in Virginia but visit Canberra, which they call home.

We were invited to Shimla for a longer time but spent only a few days and returned to Delhi to be with Aruna and Saeed. And Amrita. We went to the IIAS once more for a few days to give talks and attend a conference on the Indian Diaspora.

The journey from Delhi to Chandigarh takes around four hours by Shatabdi Express. At Chandigargh a driver and a car from IIAS were waiting for us – the driver had a placard with my name neatly printed in large letters. The drive normally should have taken three hours to reach the famous institute, but we took six: we stopped on the way for a long, leisurely lunch at a restaurant above the mountains which said CUISINE WORLD FAMOUS. The food was mediocre but the view was magnificent.

Prem Nath, the driver, sat on another table – we invited him to join us. We had our lunch, with a lot of mango juice and a beer or two. After that, he drove like a maniac, presumably feeling happy to share a meal with two foreigners at the same table. He wanted us to reach Shimla quickly on a dangerously winding road where cars, cargo lorries, and cows appeared at random. One felt one mishap could plunge you down the gorges for eternal life. The world may be maya but this reality was frightening.

We reached the IIAS in the evening and Shimla was shrouded in mist like the goonghat of a shy bride. Shimla was declared the summer capital of British India in 1864. Kipling wrote there in 1865. A rail connection was established in 1903. The Empire followed trade and missions and Shimla became the Queen of the hill stations of India.

It's a region seeped in myths and legends and kingdoms. But what strikes one most is the richness of vegetation, snow peaks and the green valleys for miles. The air is invigorating and there's a freshness that is absent in the cities on the plains.

As a student, all I remember are the people who had come mainly from Delhi to spend their holidays in this hill station. Occasionally we saw through darkly lit windows men and women enjoying themselves, unaware that a group of students were watching them with envy. Joshi and I relished our stay – the first I was experiencing in the luxury of the YMCA!

This time with Jyoti was different. We arrived to a warm welcome. One of the first persons I met on the ridge where the vice-regal building is situated was a scholar called Chetan.

He saw me and asked, 'Are you Satendra Nandan, sir?'

I was surprised and was delighted to discover that he'd written his doctoral thesis on V.S. Naipaul and me. We immediately went into a small café and had tea. Two days later, Chetan chaired my seminar with a good knowledge of my work and political interests.

IIAS is of course a premier scholarly institute. In the evening, met several scholars from all over India attending a course in translation. This is now big business in India. I recognised one familiar face from Hyderabad, a lady I'd met in Barcelona.

Next day, to my delight, I heard a familiar voice – it was my friend Harish Trivedi, a stalwart of ACLALS conferences. Harish is from Delhi University and a justly well-known scholar in Literatures in English. His wit and observations are much appreciated in ACLALS circles. Meeting Harish in Shimla was a special pleasure. We promised to see each other in Delhi on our return, but circumstances prevented us from getting together with a few friends like R.W. Desai, Deepak, Sudhir. I'm hoping to see them on my next trip to Delhi, where I hope to launch this book and meet Pankaj K. Singh, a dear friend from Shimla.

*

I think most of us take care of our physical self as we grow older; but equally important is our life of the mind. To keep it alive, curious, nimble, agile, flexible is part of one's deepest growth. Where memories mingle, 'mixing memory and desire, stirring / Dull roots with spring rain'. Except that it's winter rain slanting into the windows of your home, so close to your heart, opening and closing like those ventricles you'll never see.

Writing, then, is gardening in winter.

Friendships help us to keep ourselves healthy and healed.

For three years in Hindu College hostel, I lived among boys, some of my dearest friends as undergraduates.

And there was Dinesh Pant. Dinesh was from a well-known family

– Govind B. Pant, a minister in the Congress government, was his distant relative; Sumintranandan Pant, the poet, was another relative. But Dinesh's interests were neither in politics nor in poetry – he was more interested in playing cards and drinking military rum obtained from the soldiers. We played cards daily and the losers were supposed to cook the evening meal of chicken and rice and salad.

Except for chickens, food was cheap in the open markets – that is how India fed its millions; and no revolution was more damaging to a party in power than the rising price of onions, potatoes or tomatoes. Governments fell by these as prices rose. Crooked politicians distributed rice free at the time of elections, and the politics of plunder of one's own people often became a way of life after the elections.

Dinesh became part of our Fiji group. Soon we introduced him to a girl from Labasa – Dinesh promptly fell in love with her. His main motive I think was to get to Fiji. The young scholar returned after completing her degree. Dinesh Pant arrived in Fiji soon afterwards without any money. Luckily, we'd given him my father's home address in Legalega, next to the airport. Dinesh hired a taxi and arrived home – my father paid the taxi fare. Dinesh spent the night in our village home. The following morning, Father gave him some cash and he left for Suva, where his old friends from Delhi were now teaching.

We spent a lot of time together, and then I left for England to study. Meanwhile, Dinesh got married to his college friend. I was under the impression that she was going to marry another Fiji boy but as usual my perceptions were misplaced. I think they had two very bright children.

When I returned from my studies in England, I enquired after him. Much to my shock and horror, I was told Dinesh had perished in a road accident near Deuba. He'd been drinking with his companions and decided to drive home late at night. His car hit a stationary cargo lorry and was stuck under it. There was no one there on that lonely road to rescue him. He must have bled to death.

Dinesh Pant had died – it sounded incredible to me. He had expressed his wish to me to help him to join a political party in Fiji. And now he was dead in Fiji.

Years later in Adelaide, I met his daughter in the company of the late Dr Uma Prasad. Umanand also died in a car accident when I was in Austria.

That's how the life of my friend Dinesh ended. His wife must have migrated to Adelaide too. There are so many kinds of death, many without kindness of any kind. Dinesh's death was one of the 'most unkindest' to me personally. He'd been cut short in his prime, one of my college codgers of my card-playing days with Bhim and Narend.

*

Despite my good results in the Honours class, I was not allowed to study for my Masters – it would have given me a good grounding in modern English Lit.

But fate intervened and I found something more beautiful: my Jyoti. I saw Jyoti first in the garden of the Central Institute of Education (CIE), an institute for the training of teachers. This elegant place was situated next to Miranda House, a modern girls' college across the Delhi university café. Of all the Delhi university colleges, the Institute was perhaps best kept and maintained as it was India's premier place for the training of teachers from BEd and MEd to PhD. A few foreign students like me were admitted to it, but most of the students were selected teacher-trainees from all over India.

Jyoti had joined the CIE from Isabella Thorburn College, Lucknow, the first Asian college for Indian women founded in 1922 by an American philanthropist. The legend was that Ms Thorburn had met an Indian woman on a sea voyage and was so impressed that she decided to found a college for women in Lucknow. The designer of Canberra, where I'm writing this, Walter Burley Griffin, who died on 11 February 1937, is buried in Lucknow. He was from the USA too.

Years later, I visited the college and took all the staff of the English

Department to a lunch – it was my way of saying thank you to a place that had educated Jyoti. Indeed Jyoti's mum, aunts and the eldest sister all studied at the college, part of the University of Lucknow.

It was on the stage at the CIE that I came first to the attention of Jyoti. During the orientation week, elaborately organised at the institute, we were divided into three groups. Each group had to perform items of entertainment in the evening in front of an audience. Jyoti first beheld me performing a dance with students from Trinidad, Mauritius, Kenya and Guyana. The most remarkable feature of this dance was that most of the students were dancing to Western music. Only, it seems, I was doing my own thing without rhythm or rhyme. It was an outlandish performance, never before witnessed on an Indian stage. I'd no knowledge of Western music, having grown on goinda dances of my village, and the sad songs of Hindi films, a few of which I'd seen in Nadi. I'd never danced in my life. Fortunately, I was half-hidden at the back of the stage, behind a rather tall Kenyan girl named Saroj.

Jyoti, on the other hand, loved music and dancing in the age of Elvis the Pelvis. Elvis was a craze, I believe, but he had not touched my life; I even escaped the Beatles.

My musical talents are limited – playing a bansoori under a pandanus tree or blowing my own trumpet unnecessarily. But I do love listening to the sitar, the piano and the violin. Later in life, I was to meet both Vilayat Khan and Ravi Shankar.

My village companion Telu aka Ram Adhar, son of that mad Mangal pujari, once bought me a flute. I treasured it for years until I left Fiji for India. Years later, I met Telu in town and gave him some money in remembrance of his gift to me perhaps a couple of days of his farm wages.

Jyoti and I lived in the same hostel – the institute was residential. We ate together, attended the same classes, played on the same ground, sat on the same benches, visited the same cafés and cinemas, but slept in the different wings of the large, brick-coloured building. One Miss K. Dutt was the women's warden; one Mr M. Tuttoo was in charge of the men. Ms Dutt was a Bengali; Mr Tuttoo was a Kashmiri. Once you fall in love, you think everyone must be in love and we often wondered if those two had some liaison going.

In love, as in most things in my life, I've always been tentative and hesitant. But the tide of adolescence has its passionate boldness. My interest had hardly begun in teacher-training, when I began to notice someone had been looking at me. I hadn't noticed it before. A girl-woman shows her love in many subtle ways: sharing a fruit, licking your ice cream, drinking from the same cup, touching your hand; brushing against your body, bosom slightly bare when we sat together; perfume a bit pronounced; and numerous other magical signals. Only now I'm able to see these more vividly in the life of others. I'd no carnal knowledge: it was an age of innocence, and ignorance; adolescence seemed to have skipped by me like seasons I'd not experienced.

Mr M. Bakshi, the sports master, was enthusiastic about sports—short and stolid, he jumped from spot to spot. He made us play kabadi, a rustic game I detested. I sat on the bench and saw how the women, dressed in salwar-kameez, played the games, laughed and relaxed in the evening sun. Jyoti looked lovely to me, exceptionally beautiful in a garden surrounded by rose bushes and other girls. She wore her sporting dress in style and with elegance, her lustrous, black curly hair shining in the rays of the sun through the tall cedar trees. Her superbly shaped breasts cupped delicately in the bra showed through the thin cotton top; her dancing figure, virgin hips and buttocks, would send me into adolescent raptures: I'd read John Keats' 'The Eve of St Agnes' and now could understand the lines that made P.B. Shelley faint. Jyoti's skin had a loveliness all its own and it became luminous in the receding light of the Delhi sun.

I was falling in love.

We began having coffee together, and rasogoolas at lunch. In the CIE cafeteria, the food was excellent but a very ragged fellow served us with a dirty-looking rag flung over his left shoulder. He reminded me of one of my village companions in Legalega who used to help us on our farm. Because of that memory of Telu, I was always very gentle with him and he used to serve me first. I think he was a romantic Bengali babu at heart and must have liked both of us – a young couple in love.

Often, we sat on the benches after dinner and simply chatted about our family. Fiji must have fascinated Jyoti – so far away that it was not mentioned in any world map made in India by Atma Ram & Sons.

In the class, I sat in the back row and pretended to pay attention to the lectures. But my interest was in a beautifully dressed woman who always came a few minutes late and attracted the attention of the whole class. Many of us waited for her arrival. As the lectures began, I began writing my poems. Where I got the gift of writing poetry, I do not know. I'd written a longish poem in Form V but, once the teacher said it wasn't my work, never wrote a poem again until I went to the university. I concentrated on writing essays, which I do even to this day but it is poetry that is my joy as my love for Jyoti.

But once your heart stirs with love, poetry comes like leaves in spring, or roses in summer. Then it flowers into bad poems: one such I wrote for Jyoti. She was the most elegantly dressed woman in the college in her beautiful sarees and matching blouses. One particular saree I liked very much – blue with stars all over. I sat and wrote a poem on it, its most famous line being, 'I wish I were your saree wrapped around your waist and thighs like my sighs'.

This was subsequently bettered by Prince Charles, who wanted to be his lady's tampon! It was Charles who handed the instruments of independence to Fiji on 10 October 1970, when I was in England with my family, receiving my certificates from the elegant Duchess of Kent – she was then the chancellor of the University of Leeds.

Jyoti was handed this poem by a friend of mine at recess. She was furious by lunch. I was shocked and dismayed – a bold act of writing had made me destroy the love germinating in my heart. By dinner, I realised that Jyoti was feigning her anger – that, in fact, she was pleased and had shown it to two of our closest classmates, Saroj and Lila.

Saroj was from Kenya; Lila was from Trinidad. Four of us made a quartet of conspicuous friendship. We were always together.

Delhi taxis could take up to four people. And if you paid a couple of extra rupees, even six people could squeeze into a rather dilapidated taxi. My first experience in a Delhi taxi wasn't promising. In Fiji, taxis were the best cars and taxi drivers and lawyers' clerks ruled whatever roost there was in the Indian community among the poorest of the poor. One of my uncles owned two and he was the smartest guy in our family, with two 'wives'. I recall once four of us hired a taxi from Ajmeri gate to Regal cinema in Connaught Place. A few furlongs from the cinema, the taxi stuttered to a halt. We complained. The sardarji driver got out of the car and called another person from the roadside; together they pushed the car to the door of the cinema. I was impressed and paid the full fare to the driver. 'No problem, sar,' he'd said, and hauled the car to a repair shop nearby.

Saroj became our close friend. Lila was in love with a Guyanese chap studying at another college. The sadness is that once we left CIE, we never met until our visit to London in 1971, where an accidental encounter with a lady led me to the discovery of Saroj and her generous husband Inder Malik. Inder died last year, aged eighty-three.

One evening in September, I was sitting on the bench looking at the birds flying over tall trees to their nests. The migration of birds in the evening returning to their nests always moves me: one of my favourite poems is by Alec Hope:

> For every bird there is this last migration:
> Once more the cooling year kindles her heart;
> With a warm passage to the summer station
> Love pricks the course in lights across the chart.
> ...
> And darkness rises from the eastern valleys,
> And the winds buffet her with their hungry breath,
> And the great earth, with neither grief nor malice,
> Receives the tiny burden of her death.

I sat alone, looking melancholy, surrounded by trees and flowers in the CIE garden. I remembered those evening shadows in Fiji and the flying foxes flying towards the islands. Beyond the airport.

Jyoti must have seen me from her upstairs room. She walked across the lawn and came and sat next to me. And very gently whispered, 'I love you.'

In the descending darkness, these three words worked their magic. No one had ever said that to me, with such feeling or desire. I held her for a moment and kissed her beautiful, trembling lips. It was the first time I was kissing a woman – a rather bold act for me and perhaps a bit clumsy.

With that kiss began the longest and loveliest journey of my life. The first love is most miraculous. It's never repeated in one's lifetime. Next year it will be sixty years of love.

From that evening began our love affair: it increased in knowledge and intensity as days rolled by. We began missing lectures, tutorials, sports.

The institute was a double-storey structure. In the middle was a tower, covered with thick ivy. You could climb up the steps and reach the top: flat, spacious and quite private. Soon, we discovered it was a rendezvous spot for lovers. As we climbed the steps, occasionally a couple of senior men and women sat there chatting and possibly smooching. I think this is something that the CIE staff did not encourage but didn't discourage either. For an Indian institution of the early 1960s, it was a fairly enlightened attitude in a college.

Later, I was told several lifelong relationships began at the institute – teachers were most adept at them.

Jyoti and I met here, next to the tower, virtually every evening after dinner, when we were supposed to be studying. Mr Tuttoo made his rounds dutifully, only to be told by my senior friends that I'd gone to the university library. I think Mr Tuttoo, the tutor, was always placated if you greeted him with a polite 'sir'.

*

During the weekend, Jyoti went to her home in Motibagh, where her mother lived with her four other daughters. Motibagh was quite a distance away from CIE, in New Delhi, beyond Chanakyapuri, a residential suburb for bureaucrats and foreign embassies. Jyoti's father, a promising civil servant and a writer-critic, had attained a rather high position, having studied in Lahore, England and the US. India had gained independence barely fifteen years ago, and these civil servants worked night and day to get the country out of a most brutal vivisection in the history of imperialism: the partition.

Then one fine day, Mr Fazal Singh Nathaniel, a former air force pilot, had a massive heart attack in his office. He was rushed to the hospital but died in the evening. A chain-smoker and slightly overweight, he was barely forty-seven years old. He'd come to Delhi from Lahore. His origins are not quite clear but during partition, many, many families were separated and lost in the dust, blood and tears of this most heinous crime, generated by a ruling power and the flames fed by the fuel of communalism and the madness of religious hatred and fear. Suddenly a thousand years of living together vanished and the hatred of history was ignited by a few nefarious individuals.

Neither Gandhi nor Nehru could control the earthquake of such devastation. It was the second Mahabharat – the first was imagined; this was for real. The miracle was that during my four years stay, hardly anyone talked about it. An amnesia of massive proportions seemed to have enveloped the minds of young students. Gandhi had been assassinated on 30 January 1948, around five p.m., in the Birla House prayer garden in New Delhi. It seems a shroud had been spread over a corpse. And the face of India was hidden from us. Even the ICCR never took us to this most important spot in New Delhi where the mahatma was killed.

Pandit Nehru must have liked Fazal Nathaniel. Fazal was a reader-critic broadcasting some of his pieces in English on the AIR. I was to read them later – and Jyoti's mum gave me his golden fountain pen and his leather satchel, which I carried to Fiji as very precious possessions.

Both he and Ivy had taught at Mayo College in Rajasthan – a college for princes of all sizes and shapes. The British were good at creating these elitist institutions for the privileged and thus keeping them under obligations of all kinds. Coming from a class structure with race at its core, it was easy to see how the subjugation of the natives could be exercised through caste and colour.

Ivy was given the house, 41/C Motibagh, to stay on. She stayed in it and opened a small kindergarten school with two of her daughters and a few of her neighbours' kids. The school flourished, and when I came to know Ivy, she'd five large schools in New Delhi with around 2,000 children in her kindergarten and junior schools (English medium). Education was big business. Her three elder daughters were to teach in them from time to time: Jyoti was the best teacher, Sheilah the finest piano player and Aruna created a school-college of her own – today it's known as Vidya Niketan in Saket, with around 3,000 students up to senior forms. Whenever I visit Delhi, I give a talk to senior students there in memory of Ivy.

*

In the evening on Fridays, Jyoti used to go to Motibagh to be with her mother and four sisters, one elder, three younger. Bus number 9 passed by our institute, where we waited for it. It was always crowded and I for one never got used to the Delhi crowds and their rush to get into the already overcrowded bus. It was more like a net pulled from the ocean, loaded with fish struggling for breath.

But when Jyoti got on to the bus and waved at me, I forgot all about the discomfort and waved her my goodbye. I returned to my darkening room totally bereft. The weekend was long and lonely. I behaved like the lost hero of some Bombay film.

I loved kissing this lovely woman, with so much love for me. Every time I kissed her, her lips swelled and her radiant face gave me deep, ineffable joy. I felt her palpable love for me – we were experiencing the discovery of the springs of love hidden in the growing body of a man and a woman. Perhaps both of us were so innocent that love grew like the moon on the surging surf of the South Seas. It hung among the golden clouds and sailed among stars. It was our first love deeper than an ocean.

Then Jyoti and I were put in a play produced by Mrs Lalita Rajpal, our English lecturer. Molière's *The Would-be Gentleman* was a comedy about a rustic's desire to be a gentleman. Jyoti was Lucille and I was Cleonte, young lovers. We relished the opportunity of being together on the stage. It was, as a friend who saw the performance put it, 'Drama in real life.' He was a regular reader of the *Reader's Digest*.

But because of our love affair, our studies suffered. My assignments were often done by my friends from Hindu College; I especially remember a friend, Dev Kumar Ghatak, who acted as Brutus in the college drama I'd produced and for which our scene won the first prize. Dev created a replica of the Globe Theatre. Mr Daswani, our arts instructor, was so impressed by it that he gave me a distinction! I felt only momentarily guilty. All was foul and fair in love and art.

The academic year had teacher training practice as integral to the course. I went to Delhi Public School to teach English. Jyoti was taken to Jesus and Mary Convent; only occasionally, we observed each other's class and wrote reports.

One morning as we got ready to get into the college bus to take us to our practice teaching, Jyoti came out of the dining hall and gave me a gentle kiss. Unfortunately, Miss Damyanti Dutta was standing behind and saw this act of sacrilege with her two frustrated eyes and bulging bosom. Jyoti was summoned before the principal, another spinster. After a week, Jyoti was asked to come from home. This was cruel but we'd exceeded the bounds of decency in the eyes of some lecturers whose cultural background was the Kama Sutra.

So I began visiting her virtually every evening – I left the college around five p.m. and returned by the last bus around midnight. Studies were entirely forgotten but we did attend our lectures sitting together.

*

At Motibagh, slowly I got to know Ivy, Jyoti's mother, Sheilah, Aruna, Anupa, and Amrita. Sheilah was engaged to Rana Philip; Aruna was in love with Saeed Naqvi; Anupa and Tomi were schoolgirls at Jesus and Mary Convent. My love for Jyoti grew deeper as I got to know the family — for me the most beautiful, generous and loving family I'd met in Delhi; for that matter in India. I lost touch with my Hindu College friends.

Just before the exams, Sheilah and Rana got married. Rana's dad was living in Akbar Road, an elite residential area for senior public servants and ministers. I think he was secretary to the Ministry of Communications in the Government of India. These elite residential enclaves were created by the British with imperial intentions but now occupied by the Indians after independence. It was there, under a most resplendent and colourful Shamiana, in the spacious green lawn with flowers and Asoka trees, that I first saw and met President Radhakrishnan, the philosopher-president of India.

The patrician philosopher sat on a chair, with a large white turban embellishing his pate and looking through his rimless glasses at the world of which he was the highest votary. Later, I was to hear him and read some of his works on Indian culture and philosophy written with erudition and philosophically poetic language. After all, he was the Spalding Professor of Philosophy at Oxford before becoming the president of the Republic of India. With Pandit Jawaharlal Nehru as prime minister, Radhakrishnan as president, I couldn't think of two more extraordinary minds for the world's largest, newest and most diverse democracy, with the heritage of a mahatma. Mother India, one felt, was fortunate indeed, after the brutal vivisection of a civilisation and of millions of people. How they healed their hearts and annealed their minds to rebuild India into a nation is the most exhilarating story of the second half of the twentieth century.

Saroj and I were given a lift in one of the bridal cars with Jyoti and her sisters. We went to the church, where the wedding ceremony was held in a most elaborate and elegant hall. From there, we went to the Claridges for reception and then to Rana's home for dinner. All of them were new places for me and I was now experiencing New Delhi and its many hidden privileges.

Rana was a Syrian Christian – a most ancient and progressive community from Kerala. He had studied in Doon School and St Stephens in Delhi and was a senior executive in a large firm in Calcutta.

*

Our studies came to an end. I had to leave the hostel. I moved to Jyoti's home in Motibagh. This is normally not done in India but I was a foreigner; Jyoti's family had no man in the home. I was in love. My Fijian village philosophy was *jahan sham, wahin savera* – where you arrived in the morning, there you spent the night. This is how the girmit people survived and helped each other. I was not very distant from the many girmityas who had left India for Fiji eighty years ago in sailing ships. Many stayed in our home for days – as my aja's jehajibhais, shipmates: a most enduring mateship among the old.

Jyoti's home was becoming my home. I was happy surrounded by four loving women – Ivy, Sheilah, Jyoti, Aruna – and two schoolgirls, Anupa and Amrita. And half a dozen loyal 'sarvants'.

But often the most momentous personal decisions are made in moments. Certainly in my life fate intervened at critical times, just like the colonel in the Fiji parliament.

Jyoti's home was a happy home for me – the love and generosity in abundance that I experienced in Motibagh (literally a garden of pearls), I'd not known before. How lucky I was to have met this most generous of families in the tumultuous metropolis, wild as ocean waves on a windy day. The ancient city was full of people. Delhi became a city in my heart, because of single person, my sweetheart.

Then one day, Jyoti and I, with one of her sisters, went to Sapru

House to see Satyajit Ray's first film *Pather Panchali, Song of the Road*. It was in black and white and it was being shown as part of the Delhi Film Festival. It was an ordinary evening and we'd taken a taxi from Motibagh. My life was in full bloom, with my beloved by my side.

The hall was full of Bengalis – one could hear the percolating rhythm of the language and the agitated conversations of a very articulate community. And they were proud of their Bengali director, in some ways least like them in the parochial colonies in which many lived in Delhi. But meeting an educated Bengali was a joy and an emotional encounter for me. Pradeep Maitra at Hindu College had become my closest friend. Calcutta was a distorted sound on my grandparents' tongue. I'd not been to this city: Oh Calcutta! – city of joy and pain.

I suspect my maternal grandmother, nani, was Bangla-born. Later in life I was to meet several delightful Bengalis – writers, artists, academics, actors, students and journalists. One can only judge a person by his or her individuality and one's personal experience of the individuals. To talk of communities with one's prejudices and passions seems so primitive.

Sapru House was near Connaught Place. We arrived just in time: Jyoti, Sheilah and I. We watched the film, the first by Satyajit Ray. I'd some vague interest in films but the art of film never quite captivated my imaginative being as literature did. At Hindu College, we talked about Guru Dutt's *Kagaz ka Phool* and Charlie Chaplin's *Limelight*, two arty films with quite different visions and perspectives: one Indian, the other made by that comic cinematic genius from England.

But no film or fiction has had more immediate impact on me as *Pather Panchali*. I was twenty-two; I was deeply in love; there was always the dread that one day soon I might leave Delhi for Fiji. And separation would be unbearable. Love is another word for immortality.

After the film, I recall, we got a taxi home. Throughout the winding, darkened streets around midnight, I lay my head in Jyoti's lap and wept. Tears shook my heart inconsolably. I was a sentimental bloke from the village of Votualevu. Jyoti couldn't understand my uncontrollable grief.

I couldn't communicate to my love the pain and memories of childhood that Ray had captured so poignantly and exquisitely in black and white – his first film. Few in Delhi, I felt, could understand the song of the little gifts of life – a fallen fruit, seeing a train passing, or visiting an old, emaciated auntie sitting neglected in a corner of such human distress and physical dereliction. That was the humane power of inimitable art. The joys in the hearts of children and the desolation in the adults communicated the deepest of the human condition.

And a simple pandit father, dependent on others, dreaming to be a writer, and their more complex mother with her dreams and daily humiliations in such abject poverty touched my spirit. Suddenly the familiar past became an obsessive present with the poignancy of memory.

In the Ray film, I suddenly saw the trodden, sodden paths of Maigania and Votualevu and Legalega, the village by the airport. Ray had captured in that unique world the most universal of human experience: childhood in its little joys and longings in that harsh world, wherein humanity was only fitfully glimpsed on the sad song of the road where yesterday's footprints are washed away by a few drops of rain. And like the earth, we renew ourselves every morning.

It hit me deep in my guts as if it mirrored the story of my family in their huts, broken bures, lean-tos covered with unpainted sheets of corrugated iron, and crudely cut coal-tar drums for walls. The morning sun's rays came through the chinks, as did the afternoon rain.

The story, the images, the lethal dailiness of living, reminded me of my sisters and brothers. Three of them had married; three younger ones were at home with my parents in Legalega. My mother's image floated across my mind; my father sitting having his tea in the morning in the shade of a half-broken bure, leaning precariously. The tattered homes, the few utensils, the roughly swept aangan, the neighbours, cruel and compassionate, the mother's dreams of a better life in another world, the simplicity of the father; the old woman like nani waiting for her meals if only someone served her; the eternal cow eternally chewing its cud like Lali; the calf, the lily pond and its insects dancing on the surface of the water; the well and the coconut palms; the passing, satanic locomotive and the children's first sight of it and the smell of its smoke – we'd felt it in our nostrils on the pakkilines of Maigania and Namoli. And our games with bows and arrows for we'd been to Ramlila in our village of Votualevu, where Rajbali pandit thundered the shlokas and we, his monkeys – banar sena – made mischief to delight the crowd for a fortnight. Our evenings were lit by such activities. Then we'd plenty of time to stand and stare, play and pray.

No work of art had affected me so deeply – the images, the music, the cinematography and above all the story, epic in its ordinariness, moved me with a force I'd not imagined. The details were taken from our daily lives from the many villages of Fiji where the girmit people had made their homes, thousands of miles away. The unseen grandeur of any ordinary day.

The monsoon, the winds, the dilapidated homes, the few characters of the village, the meanness of a small place, the kindness of some, and the heartbreaks of life all contained on this most human and universal of poems – the Song of the Road. I'd walked on that road; I knew the poverty of my parents; the sorrows of my mother; the love of my brothers and sisters and the dreams that bobbed up and down like empty tins in the waters of Mangal's lake and Kalpu's kund.

Food we always had in abundance; but material possessions were not part of our lives. Hori's young daughter stealing guavas for her father's very old sister, or a piece of jewellery from a rich neighbour's house. For us, the fruits grew on wild guava trees and pawpaws rotted on the stems of trees. Coconuts fell in nani's orchard of twenty-four trees, swaying in the sea breeze.

Vignettes of childhood imprisoned in each frame with such resonance that I felt I was witnessing the days and nights of my childhood with my sisters, brothers and village companions I'd left behind in their little quarrels and petty jealousies. Even Durga and Apu munching stolen sugar cane sticks, while waiting for the passing train with its black smoke billowing across the pristine landscape, becomes a powerful premonition of the disasters to follow. Images of butterflies, the insects dancing before the monsoon deluge and the occasional visiting performers, reminded me of our Ram Lila days and festivals we celebrated in the poorest of homes. Except that we didn't know we were so poor; or rather that others were so rich.

Hori, the dreamer pandit, who wants to be a writer, finally does get a decent job in another town; he has to leave his family of three. Months later, he returns to his broken home with gifts. But his world had been devastated by a storm; and he has lost his most precious gift of all: Durga, his daughter, is dead.

You'll hardly ever see a more heartrending scene than when the tragedy hits his heart. The music of Ravi Shankar tears the very heart of sorrow and grief becomes transcendent. The reality of life is ripped open but no blood flows. That is death.

At the end, Apu is alone. The world darkens as the child experiences death and sorrow in his poor but once-happy family. He begins to sense that there are other darker monsoons to come – one had taken his beloved sister away from him.

Finally, the family leave their ancestral abode on a bullock cart: with their few belongings, they leave the ancient village to go to Benaras – mother, father and young Apu. How often the people of Fiji have made this journey – from those forgotten villages of India to the islands; from the islands, scarred but not broken, to the mainlands of metropolitan societies. The brokenness of life litters the little roads on which we journey – often alone.

*

Suddenly that summer, I left Jyoti and Delhi. We promised each other with tears, long after everyone was asleep, we'd stay away for five years. One fine morning, two of my friends – Deepak and Rajinder – came to Palam airport to see me fly off to Fiji. Jyoti also came in her mum's car. I do not know what I said or what we did.

This was my saddest flight to Fiji. I was leaving Jyoti in Delhi alone but we were young; there was hope in our hearts that we'd meet again. Now, years later, I find it difficult to think how I left my Jyoti so suddenly – how sad her young heart must have been that day. Fiji was far away and we might never see each other again.

How could I have left her in Delhi all by herself, waiting for a few years? We'd said five – it's not long when you're barely in your early twenties. My grandparents had travelled to Fiji for five years but remained on the lonely islands until their death. It's also true that I hadn't quite realised the loneliness and ache of being in love when one cannot touch the beloved.

In life, things happen that will break your heart or fever your brain. But there is a comfort in the strength of love.

There're things that you experience that now when you look back, you can only sing 'I'll be Loving you Eternally' – I had heard it in Charlie Chaplin's *Limelight* – but I had grown up on Guru Dutt's *Kagaz ke Phool* and *Pyasa*. Guru Dutt committed suicide: he, too, was in love.

Within a year, I was back in Delhi, the city of my heart, with my sweetheart. And then I knew how deeply this woman loved me – it's been like that for the past sixty years.

One can only thank one's lucky stars for things that are as close to one's eyes and, at times, as distant as the stars. My beautiful wife went through coups and all kinds of human sorrows, away from her home in Delhi, but we lived, loved and travelled together, and suffered the slings and arrows of our outrageous fortunes. Often, like so many, we came close to dying and betrayal, exile and return, love and life.

There are blessings in life which make you want to bless others.

I do not think anyone would have loved me more than my Jyoti, the loving light of my life.

3. The House That Ivy Built

The house was to be demolished by a rich builder: a new four-storey building was to be erected in its place, wrote Amrita. Among her sisters, she, the youngest, has lived the longest in that Delhi home.

I felt a pang of aching nostalgia in a corner of my ageing heart. It ached for things that are no more – some things you can see floating in the misty river of time towards a restless, insatiable ocean of memories. All I can do is to sit by the river in a flood of tears in the sands of remembrances. But Jyoti is with me and that is joy enough.

The house was built by Ivy in 1966, when she was sixty years old. Her first structure searching for permanence of a kind. A widow and mother of five beautiful women, she had lived in rented homes since her civil servant husband died suddenly while at work.

The house is close to Safdurjung Hospital where Indira Gandhi's bullet-ridden body lay for hours before she was declared dead to the shock of the world: the second Gandhi to be assassinated in New Delhi by the people she trusted as her bodyguards. She was a tough woman with a fragile body: how the steel bullets must have rent her silk saree, satin blouse. Next to the hospital is a small airport where Indira's son Sanjay perished in the crash of a self-piloted small aircraft. Not far from Ivy's house is the place where Mahatma Gandhi was assassinated on 30 January 1948.

These deaths for me had some connections –Indira Gandhi was assassinated on 31 October, Ivy's birthday, in 1984. Sanjay had studied in the Doon School where I had taught later: one of my brothers-in-law, Rana Philip from Kerala, was his schoolmate; another, Saeed Naqvi from Lucknow, was his friend. Rana and Sheilah in Rana's retirement lived in Bangalore; Saeed writes his weekly column from Delhi after a world-renowned career in the TV program *World Report*, akin to *Foreign Correspondent* of the ABC. Few journalists have travelled more than Saeed Naqvi in search of interesting stories, especially in the Indian diaspora from girmit to more recent cosmopolitan migration. For decades, he produced a remarkable series for *World Report* on Doordarshan. He was possibly India's finest foreign correspondent on TV. I've scarcely known an Indian who knows India as intimately as Saeed Naqvi and has a more inquisitive curiosity of the world. Saeed visited Fiji three times and was the first journalist to do an in-depth interview with our local colonel after the coups in 1987. Aruna, Saeed's wife and Jyoti's younger sister, runs a most progressive educational institution in New Delhi.

It was at Aruna-Saeed's home that I met some of the most remarkable artists of music, writers of literature, actors and poets, and many a defeated politicians and political pundits, including Mark Tully of BBC fame.

Mrs Rabin, the slain Israeli PM's wife, had also come to dinner at Aruna-Saeed's Sainik Farm home: when she saw me, she said with a smile, 'I thought you were Peter Arnett of CNN' – at that time a most familiar face on TV screens all over the world with an intelligent and telling pate. He was, I believe, a Kiwi.

But Mrs Gandhi had another connection with Fiji: she was the only Indian prime minister who came, on her way from Australia, to Fiji in 1982 and opened the Girmit Centre in Lautoka in the sugar fields, close to Field 40, next to the avenue of huge rain trees planted by my paternal girmit grandfather, my aja. He whispered that to my father as his son drove him to Lautoka hospital where he died in the evening.

The people of Fiji gave Indira Gandhi an unforgettable welcome. I was asked to read a poem, 'The Ghost', in a Hindi translation in front of two prime ministers: Ratu Kamisese Mara from Fiji and Shrimati Indira Gandhi from India. My mother, sitting in the front row, felt truly proud.

We'd gathered together around 100 girmityas from many parts of

Viti Levu at the centre. After the then leader of the opposition Mr Jairam Reddy's speech, Mrs Gandhi greeted each one of them as if they were the lost fragments of India's heart. My mother told her village friends later in the evening that she saw the two prime ministers crying as I read my poem.

'That's what bad poetry does even to PMs!' my young doctor brother commented.

But no cynical comment could dim my mother's pride in her son's poem about her mother and father, my nani and nana, two girmityas who had arrived in Fiji around the turn of the century. Nani, our mother's mother, was our favourite Indian from Mother India.

By sheer coincidence, I've written three pieces on the death of Nehru, Indira and Rajiv. I was teaching in Doon School when Pandit Nehru died; I was in Fiji when Indira was shot; I was in Canberra when Rajiv was blown to bits by a suicide bomber. The terrible death bulletin of Rajiv was delivered to me by my son Rohan – I can still hear the shock and grief in the timbre his young voice. I have visited the nondescript obscure place where he was killed so brutally.

We'd a memorial service at the ANU where I spoke. The then Indian high commissioner in Australia sent my speech to Mrs Sonia Gandhi, and the following year, on Republic Day at the Indian High Commission in Canberra, I was presented with two beautifully published volumes on Rajiv Gandhi's life, signed by his widowed wife. I've treasured these volumes with a special understanding of love and loss in the heart of a woman, a wife, a mother, a widow. That she was from another country made me sadder still, for one can feel very lonely in India. And she'd married her Indian rather young.

*

The Girmit Centre was created to commemorate the centenary of Indian arrival into Fiji, 1879–1979. I was closely involved in its conception and collection of funds with a few other very enthusiastic Indian businessmen and public-spirited individuals like Y.P. Reddy, Dick Singh, Navin Maharaj, Dalpat Rathod and Ram Vilash. Ratu Mara and the then governor-general, Ratu Penaia Ganilau, supported the idea of a memorial to the girmityas with a donation of fourteen acres of prime Crown land and $150,000.

Many men and women gave generously to this hallowed memory of around 60, 000 mainly peasant migrants brought from India to Fiji, under the indenture system. The collected funds were kept in trust by Y.P. Reddy, Ram Vilash and Dick Singh. The first section of the centre was built, which Mrs Gandhi had opened in front of several thousands of Fiji people. Then came the coups.

Now, the centre looks desolate and neglected, with an occasional meetings held in its compound. Many of the rain trees, like girmityas, have been felled to widen the road to the harbour and the sugar city Lautoka.

Even academics were indifferent to the historical monument with its original concept of a place to study the Indian diasporic story of many strands beyond the South Pacific. It could be a university centre for research, arts, history and writing with the wings of a museum and a library for the children of Western Viti Levu, to begin with. So I'd envisioned in my project proposal which the PM of Fiji had apparently liked.

I entered the Fiji parliament in 1982 and again in 1987. Then the colonel's coup on 14 May 1987. The centre stands a silent, shipwrecked monument to the great silence of the girmit people. During the 2000 coup, it gave shelter to the displaced and dispossessed refugees from beyond Suva.

*

I'd been given a scholarship to study in Delhi. I graduated with honours in the early 1960s and was given an award to complete the BEd degree to be a trained teacher. It was at the Central Institute of Education,

India's premier institution for the training of teachers and educational research up to doctoral studies. In the most salubrious atmosphere in an educational institution in old Delhi, I met Ivy's beautiful second daughter Jyoti, who became my college sweetheart. We fell in love and life changed radiantly for me. Until then, I was a studious student doing quite well in my exams and doing the homework of a few college mates. Now, my college mates did my homework: neither Jyoti nor I cared for our university work. Love was all and being loved was more than all.

Jyoti's father Fazal was a Christian and had studied in Scotland and the US. Born in Lahore, he had lost his parents and was presumably educated by a Christian mission. He had come to Delhi after his marriage to Ivy. After that most heinous crime of imperialism – the vivisection of India, done with indecent speed and shameful flight – the displaced lived in tents and made a divided new nation with ancient roots amidst the chaos of partition's mayhem.

Millions were caught in the maelstrom of madness of men who had survived together for a millennium and, despite communal strife, had created most marvellous works of art, literature, architecture, music, festivals of the joy of living. Life despite its poverty and cruelty of castes was exalted in the beauty of India's people, so giving – which I experienced in a family or two.

During the chaos of partition, so much changed and from the dawn emerged an immense darkness.

One evening, a mob came to lynch Fazal. He'd a Muslim-sounding name – Urdu was the common language of poetry and culture; Lahore, the birthplace of Fazal, was the crucible of that culture. Fazal, his parents must have thought, had a beautiful meaning. As the mob rioted in front of the house, young Ivy came out with a Bible in her hand and assured the menacing mob that her husband was a Christian. She swore on her black Bible and the mob was pacified and left her family alone. I do not think she ever travelled anywhere without her holy Bible in her bag. And her first gift to everyone she cared for was a copy of the Bible signed by her. She believed in its words implicitly with an unshakable faith and an incandescent personal conviction. Jyoti keeps her mother's grey cloth-covered Bible in our bedroom.

Then Gandhi was assassinated on 30 January 1948, at five seventeen p.m. in the prayer garden of Birla House. All the six-year-old Jyoti remembers is seeing her bereaved father in the home garden with tears rolling down his face as Gandhi's funeral cortège wound its way to Rajghat on the banks of the Yamuna river for cremation the following day. In Delhi, I've visited this hallowed ground many times but it took me a long time to visit Birla House, where Mohandas Karamchand Gandhi was killed with three bullets from the pistol of a man whose surname was Godse.

And Gandhi died with two words: 'Heh Ram! Oh God.'

*

With her three older daughters and a few children from the neighborhood, Ivy started her first kindergarten in the government quarters at Motibagh. She was allowed to stay in C2 quarters for more than two decades, apparently on the instructions of Pandit Nehru. As her school flourished, she was given permission to build a school on the available land for the children of the locality. Motibagh school became the main source of Ivy's income.

Occasionally, someone envious of Ivy's educational success would place an idol in the midst of the school tents but no one bothered her or doubted the quality of the education the children received in her schools from kindergarten to class six. One night, a rival group burned down her tents in Motibagh. Next morning, Ivy was there erecting new and bigger tents for the children of the school. The school flourished, as if blessed by some supernatural power: Ivy started three more schools in different 'colonies' of New Delhi.

I do not think Ivy ever lost faith in her God. I acquired some knowledge of the Bible through her but she never insisted that I become a Christian before marrying her Christian daughter. Love, she understood, was deeper than faith and where there's love a greater presence is always there, coupled with a mother's blessings.

It was from Motibagh that Sheilah, the eldest, got married to Rana in a resplendent ceremony. For me, it was the first Delhi wedding of the kind I was invited to with my college friend Saroj Kapila from Kenya.

The chief guest was President Radhakrishnan, sitting in the middle of the colourful shamiana in Akbar Road, looking very presidential, with a white philosophical turban. And Rana's father, Mr Philip Modayil, telling me, 'Barkis is willing', a reference to a character in Dickens's *David Copperfield* much in love with the young David's relation. He wanted me to repeat that message-mantra every time I met Jyoti!

Rana's father was a very senior public servant and I remember him as a kindly, literate man. His mother was a lady of great dignity – both were from Kerala and Syrian Christians. It's a pity I didn't get to know them or spent more time with them.

India was too big for me and I'd come from a little obscure village in Fiji – perhaps more remote than the villages from which my grandparents had migrated to Fiji. It must have been such a long journey of longings for them, a journey from the hinterland of a subcontinent into some of the tiniest islands in the largest ocean, the blue Pacific. My imagination was still tied to villages and islands.

After their marriage, Rana-Sheilah moved to Calcutta where Rana had a lucrative position in a large firm, INDAL. I wish I'd visited Calcutta when they were there. As it happens, I've never really been to Calcutta from where my peasant grandparents, all four of them, boarded their sailing ships to the South Seas, never to return. I was the first to build a rainbow bridge from Nandi to New Delhi, almost eight decades later. And when Jyoti came to Nadi with me at Christmas 1965, the circle was complete in a sense but the historical darkness at the centre remained unexplored, and unununderstood by my generation. Now I marvel at my fathomless ignorance.

But love is love – where innocence and experience come together. And the fruit from the tree of knowledge, once eaten, brings you into the worlds of agony and ecstasy.

I returned to Fiji in 1963 and began teaching at my alma mater but my heart was in Delhi. I returned to Motibagh within a year, after a most memorable farewell at SVHS. It was a year of friendships for me so deeply cherished by so many of my students and colleagues. But I missed Jyoti infinitely. That year of teaching gave me a couple of life-long friendships, including Suresh Tappoo, a writer friend and a patron of literary productions. His younger brother Mahendra is also an artist of considerable talent. That one year at my old secondary school was deeply happy for me in my aching loneliness and I spent most of my time writing love letters to Jyoti in Delhi.

In July 1963, I returned to Delhi.

*

In Delhi, Jyoti and I got married in a big, beautiful shamiana with shehnai music in the Motibagh park in front of Ivy's home on 27 September 1963. I had, a few months before our marriage, been appointed an English teacher at the Doon School, Dehradun, just below the Mussourie hill station. Ivy and her two younger daughters stayed at Motibagh. Aruna-Saeed, too, had got married and had a baby, Saba. According to both, it was a virgin birth, whatever that meant. But Saeed was often heard tiptoeing for glasses of milk after the midnight hour.

After a year, Ivy moved to South Extension and rented a large upstairs flat. Jyoti and I lived in Chestnut House in Doon School. During mid-semester breaks, I went on treks with students and staff across rocky terrains, streams, mountains and rugged landscapes in the Himalayan foothills. Jyoti went to Delhi to be with her mother and sisters. Our camping trips with the young students were well-organised, and we travelled for the unfathomed beauty of the valleys, the majesty of the peaks glowing golden-grained in the setting sun.

I now wish I'd understood the meanings of those mountain treks into the most pristine wilderness. My mind was not trained for such luxuries and I didn't take full advantage of the life-enriching experience with my students and colleagues. One or two, like Hari Dang and Gurudyal Singh, had been part of the Indian Everest expeditions, adding prestige to the famous public school situated in the most beautiful forest station with tall trees and green cricket pitches – an idyllic setting amidst mountains and winding roads. But even there we were not reading about the trees and mountains of India – we were still engrossed in the texts of English literature and entertained by the manners and mores of English life.

I missed the wonder and beauty of mountains from the foothills of which my ancestors had migrated to the islands of the South Seas.

Travelling from Dehradun to Delhi by train was a joy. We loved the night journey by Dehradun Express to Delhi railway station, where Ivy's car was always waiting for us as if we'd come from some other country. We arrived at Ivy's breakfast table with the real happiness of a loving home.

In the summer of 1964, Ivy visited us with her two sisters, Nancy and Pansy. Nancy was a tall, handsome lady, Victorian and very dignified. Pansy was less formidable and more human. In the evenings, we used to go with baskets to collect lychees from trees growing on the outskirts of the school. Our residence, Chestnut House, was covered with ivy leaves with a large balcony from which we could see the lights of Mussourie glimmering like distant stars. Personally, I did not quite appreciate the richness of life in the Doon School and its extraordinary ambience for the young students and its new teachers who came after graduation; after a year or two, they disappeared in some tea estates of Assam or in some firm as executives.

An Indian public school, like its model in England, I think, had a whiff of gay culture of sorts and the principal, Mr J.A.K. Martyn, was perhaps more understanding than his senior Indian teachers. Many appeared too traditional and conservative to me. It was at Doon that I met King Hussein of Jordan – he'd come to see his old teacher at Harrow, Mr Martyn. Another renowned visitor to the school was Zakir Hussein, the president of India. And one of my students was Vikram Seth, now a well-known writer. I also produced *Julius Caesar*; Vikram was Cinna the poet: 'Tear him for his bad verses!' when he's mistaken for Cinna, one of the conspirators.

*

After a year's honeymoon, Jyoti and I returned to Delhi with Jyoti pregnant with Rohan and I'd become a fairly decent tennis player. We stayed with Ivy and then shifted to a rented flat owned by a crooked landlord named Khanna. He took several thousand rupees in advance and gave us a mediocre flat and, when we didn't want it, the crook wouldn't return the advance.

So Saeed-Aruna, Jyoti and I shared the flat and, since it was in South Extension, close to Ivy's flat, most of our meals were at Ivy's, prepared by Muleram. Often, Mummy would invite a dozen or so Fijian students for lunch or dinner on Sundays – I think she'd a special affection for people away from their parents and home. I was lucky to have such a mother-in-law, in fact more a mother, who understood the loneliness of some of us in Delhi. But what of her widowed sorrows?

*

It was some time in 1965 that the vacant land with green grass, a few stray cows grazing under the trees behind the Safdurjung Hospital, was being auctioned. Ivy and I went to the auction every morning for three days. Our bid for a piece of land was always exceeded by some other businessman, much wealthier than Ivy. Finally, at the end of the third day, as the sun was setting and kites darkened the sky, our last bid of Rs 58,065 for a plot was accepted.

Some people present said, 'Mataji has been here for three days. Let her have that plot.'

I was moved by this Indian compassion for a woman.

Ivy, too, was overwhelmed by the generosity of the Delhi businessmen. We rushed out of the auction tent to see the plot in the dust of dusk. The plot allotted to us was the last one, next to a nullah, open and wide. It seems no one else wanted it. We hadn't even seen it before bidding for it. Life's been a bit like that for me ever since – doing things without seeing! This is often mistaken for my vision. I'd say muddling through life but with a lot of love and a bit of luck.

We rushed back to the auctioneers and tried to return the plot. It was a triangular one with an eroding soil bank. Ivy finally had to purchase it, even if she was disappointed by the site at first sight.

The noise of DTU buses belching smoke and occasional flame was only about 300 metres from the plot. Across the wide but shallow ravine were government quarters for the Indian bureaucracy, constructed, it seemed, by indifferent contractors, without any aesthetics in their architecture.

I liked the open park, hoping one day it would be a park full of tress and children playing cricket and old men dozing in the winter sun and ayahs strolling with little children, holding their hands. The peanut-seller with his warm angithi would supply the nuts for a few annas, keeping us feeling warm, with peanuts and channa in massala. And corn on the cob garnished with lemon and spices.

On occasions, we saw an elephant decked in colour marching majestically on the Zhandu Singh Road towards the large Deer Park, led by a noisy, comically coloured band-baja. Across the nallah, the music played for everybody's entertainment and recitals of Hindu hymns and film songs on some celebrations echoed late into the night. That these noises might disturb a sick child or a dying old person didn't seem to bother anyone. There was some connection, I feel, in throwing the kachra in the nallah and the noise across it: an absence of a civic sense or consideration for the Other. Or perhaps it gave some musical order to the general chaos of life.

*

After a year at Doon School, I began training as a journalist at *The Statesman*; Jyoti was teaching in one of Ivy's schools. By now, she'd five, with around four thousand children from kindergarten to class six. Ivy's schools were all English medium with very smart teachers, mainly wives of civil servants; they didn't need the money but some preoccupation daily for half a day away from 'sarvants' and mothers-in-law. Ivy was the manager and the principal of all the schools and visited every school in her Ambassador car. Sometimes we went with her to meet the teachers and talk to the pupils. Ivy had created the schools and one could see her pride in running them so professionally. Every teacher seemed happy to be in her schools. Ivy was the most popular, principal-manager.

Although none of her daughters or sons-in-law took any particular interest in the schools, it was through the earnings of the school that Sheilah went to London to study music and all Ivy's daughters got higher education in celebrated colleges.

Aruna finally did create one of Delhi's more renowned schools named Vidya Niketan in Saket. On every visit to Delhi, we visit Aruna's co-educational school with very progressive ideas for a new India.

Both Ivy and Jyoti's dad had started their careers as teachers in Mayo College, Ajmer in Rajasthan, a rather opulent and gaudy place meant for numerous princelings of Rajasthan.

Subsequently, Fazal was selected for and joined the Indian Civil Service, ICS: a huge bureaucracy created by the Raj to oil the machinery of Empire; it may even have prevented a recently partitioned India from sliding into a deeper chaos. But few talked about this abominable imperial crime and religious fanaticism: a modern Mahabharata – an epic that diminished the idea of a greater world that Vyasa's great epic had imagined in most holocaustic ways. Every epic is about a local quarrel in the mind of men and women wherein blood-madness flows in bloody battles of a body tearing itself apart.

My career at *The Statesman* didn't blossom as my humzulf Saeed's. He flourished as a journalist; I remained a university graduate playing cards and loving my Jyoti. After a stint at *The Statesman*, Principal Din Dayal invited me as a senior teacher of English at the Delhi Public School. Mr Din Dayal became very fond of me and gave me all kinds of opportunities to go further in my profession, obtaining a British Council bursary to train as an English teacher in London. But I was too much in love to worry about a career or to understand the opportunities open to me through this most generous of men, tall as a palm tree. I didn't take up the British Council offer.

My two young sisters-in-law, Anupa and Amrita, continued their secondary education at Jesus and Mary Convent: Anupa a first-class student; Amrita full of teenage angst. The contrast between the two sisters was marked. Amrita became a well-known editor and writer in Delhi.

Rohan, our son, was born on 22 September 1964. He was the first male child in the family after three generations: Jyoti's grandmothers were sisters; Jyoti's mum had two sisters, and many cousins, all women; Ivy gave birth to five daughters; Aruna-Saeed had a daughter, Saba.

Life had acquired a rhythm: I was beginning to enjoy Delhi as a householder without knowing Delhi's galis and the demands of a metropolis burgeoning in every direction. Some of my friends had chosen business careers – an area of deepest darkness for me. I got to know through Mummy a remarkable couple, Mr and Mrs Chib. Mr Chib was the director-general of Indian tourism and a dear friend of Fazal and Ivy. After Fazal's untimely death, he assisted Ivy in many ways. When Mr Chib retired, he took a position in the Bahamas, the first archipelago Columbus touched in the Caribbean in 1492.

I'm told Mr Chib transformed the tourist industry in that part of the world as he'd done in India. He was a Cambridge-educated man and sent his two children, Pappu and Kaka, to Cambridge to study: Pappu and Kaka, good friends of Saeed and Aruna, Rana and Sheilah. Mrs Chib was a dear family friend and very fond of Ivy, although in their personalities they were worlds apart.

*

Then one fine day, just before Christmas, Jyoti and I decided to go to Fiji with Rohan. Jyoti was expecting another child. We arrived in Nadi in December 1965 and stayed in my village for Christmas until I got a position as an English teacher in Suva in January 1966. Compared to Ivy's rented flat with servants, my village home was a manger. There was no electricity or water supply or flush toilet. The well near our tin and timber house was the source of more than water. My parents had done their best to make it as comfortable as they could for their daughter-in-law from India. And Jyoti, after a few hiccups, showed her character and understanding and, above all, her love for me. She, I think, understood more than I could ever imagine. I doubt if anyone from Fiji had ever gone to Delhi from a poorer family. But Jyoti's love transcended all the limitations of my village in Votualevu and my family's resources. And my ignorance of life matters in general.

Soon, I was appointed head of English at a college in Suva. We moved to Suva and rented Master Lal Singh's flat in Bureta Street, near Kundan Singh's shop.

Gitanjali was born in CWM on 9 February. After a few months, Jyoti, too, began her career as an English teacher in a neighbouring secondary school named after Mahatma Gandhi.

We stayed in Suva for a year in Master Lal Singh's house. He was a primary school headteacher and rented his 'whole house' to us but lived downstairs on weekends. After a year when I accumulated heavy debts and a new friend helped me pay them, we decided to go back to Nadi, a cheaper town and nearer to my ancestral homes in Maigania and Legalega. In February 1967, Mr P.N.D. Moosad, another remarkable man from Kerala, invited me to join SVHS school. I became the head of English at my alma mater in Nadi. Jyoti joined the school next to our rented flat owned by a shopkeeper named Pala.

In my second year at Shri Vivekananda, the USP opened as a university. I was offered the job of lecturer in English, which surprised more than me, for I'd only an Indian degree in English and Fiji had many expatriates and locals trained in New Zealand, Australia and England. An application written in a shop and posted by my shopkeeper pal brought this luck for me. It was an important breakthrough in my life and career. I'd an opportunity to join the civil service but declined, in order to further my education. That choice has made an immense difference to me personally and to my family generally.

We arrived back in Suva and had a beautiful house on the grounds of the Laucala campus of USP, which was originally a seaplane base for the New Zealand air force. The view of the Pacific from the top of the campus was simply stunning: you could also see the Nukulau island where the indentured were first quarantined before they were distributed among the sugar estates of the CSR company. The hill and river people were stranded in the middle of the Pacific Ocean on the smallest island, near Suva Point.

*

Ivy had not travelled outside India, but to see her daughter, she visited Fiji with sarees for Jyoti and Indian mangoes hidden in her overweight suitcase. Meanwhile, her house was being built in Delhi, designed by Satish Grover, a friend of Saeed and Aruna. Ivy needed a break and she came to Fiji to see her daughter and two grandchildren. Ivy loved Jyoti. Fiji, she said, was a blessed Christian country, although she was intrigued by the topa the native Fijians were wearing!

She travelled to the two villages I'd grown up in and stayed with my family. Soon, she made contact with the church people and went preaching with them. Even my father attended a few times in the evenings. We were so happy she'd come all the way to see us in Fiji – I think it was her first trip outside India. She spent some time in my village homes and had a natural empathy for ordinary people. A picture taken with my mother in our village home remains a precious memento in our family album. But my mother's world and Ivy's were different geographically and emotionally. More than two oceans lay between them but the bonding of two mothers was also present.

*

After a month with us in Viti Levu, Ivy returned to Delhi to her new house at A-1/177 Safdurjung Enclave. It was a three-storey building, the most elegantly designed structure on that street. The ground flat was rented. On the first floor, Ivy lived with her two daughters. In the barsati lived her driver, named Samson; at the other end of the barsati was a hall for Christian visitors from many parts of the world, especially Canada and the USA, especially Sisters Alice and Ruth; even pastor Nathaniel from Fiji via the US stayed at Ivy's home for months. They were all preachers and evangelists on a mission. But Ivy's home was their anchor and they stayed as long as they wished. Ivy had experienced both the blessing and the grace of her Lord. She was closest to Sister Alice, who tried her best to convert us to her belief but to no avail. From Delhi, she often went to Pakistan. And through Alice's brother in Canada, Ivy always sent us money for more than Christmas gifts.

A friend of mine from Fiji, Hari Prasad, stayed for several months in the house in Delhi. He had given me in 1966 a remarkable book, *The Strangled Cry* by John Strachey, published in 1962, which I have to this day in my library. He had gone in search of a bride, preferably a dancer, but poor chap wasn't a dancer himself. I felt a bit sad for him as he'd helped me in Suva; today, I do not know where he is but I often think of his kindness to me during that year of living beyond my means.

Adjacent to Safdurjung, a few blocks away, was a small bazaar, dirty, dusty with an open sewage system. But it met almost all the needs of the locality and we often sent Samson to get things which we suddenly needed. Sometimes, I accompanied Samson just to see the life of the bazaar in the shadows of the most richly constructed and colorfully decorated buildings with the strange names of the owners. In Fiji, I was more used to the fancy names of film stars but the surnames in Safdurjung on the plates made no sense to me; they were strange and alien. But it was I who was the alien.

In the evenings, we saw very elegantly dressed men and women taking a stroll towards the bazaar totally oblivious of the soggy conditions bleeding below their chappals. I found it difficult to understand this indifference to the obvious as if there was no awareness of municipal responsibilities.

*

Ivy's home upstairs, with three marbled attached bathrooms and toilets to three spacious bedrooms, gave all of us a feeling of belonging. There were a few precious things: near the dining table, an old, faded print of the Last Supper hung forlornly on the wall; in the lounge, above the ancient black telephone, the picture of Jesus, the silent guest at every conversation and meal. A few decorated plates were placed on the walls. A piano was in a corner with an attractively carved stool for the piano player.

As years passed, the material comforts became less important to Ivy but we as children became dearer to her, I feel, especially Jyoti, who was physically farthest from her mum, but closest to her heart.

The architect had left an open space in the middle of the house where a shaft of light came down to illuminate the kitchen on the ground floor through a rectangular open space. We lived on the first: that was Mummy's home. Both the back and the front had balconies – rather narrow ones – but we were able to sit on cane chairs and morahs and have dry nuts in the winter sunshine.

Ivy bought heaps of nuts from the INA market not far from the house. The market was full of fruits, vegetables, daily utensils, fish and fowl. A multitude of vendors in colourful clothes making noises to sell their wares – a genuine Indian bazaar, with its seeming teeming confusion but beneath a carefully organised system. As we munched nuts and channas, Shanti, the ever complaining but faithful woman, oiled Mummy's gorgeous hair and malished her feet.

I do not think any of her daughters have Ivy's gloriously grey head of hair or the pure tenderness and luminosity of her skin. Her upbringing in Rajasthan, with its unadulterated food, clean water and fresh air, and her sporting prowess, gave Ivy a vitality unknown in Delhi's polluted, overpopulated colonies.

From the back balcony, we could see an incomplete house in its rough concrete. Apparently, the businessman building a huge house went bankrupt midway and the house remained half-built for years. The unfinished structure was an eyesore but we didn't mind it until we saw the neighbours throwing their kura near its half-constructed walls. We made up most fantastic stories about the builder – murders and rapes in Delhi were not uncommon. Someone even suggested the wretched man had murdered and buried his wife in the foundation of the structure.

Beyond the incomplete building, kites circled in the dust of Delhi's wintry sky, and not a patch of blue visible anywhere. We waited for our meals and meetings among the windy spaces and embraces of our old relations who visited Ivy from other towns and cities. We waited for the monsoon to clean up the garbage-clogged nallah.

The balcony also gave us a vista of the backyard – often called in Delhi 'the backside'. The nullah flowed like cold lava but the monsoon washed away the accumulated debris like some antibiotic clearing the cough in a rattling throat. People from across began throwing their kura-karkat and the nallah looked suffocated. Civic sense seemed alien to these rich banias and civil servants, as someone defined them with disgust.

A few trees grew big and green while pigs and goats roamed foraging for food in the bush that invaded the banks of the nallah. Sometimes, human buttocks were glimpsed among the bush, half hidden. Once, I saw a crow riding on a pig's back and I used that image in my poem 'Hope in Delhi' as a metaphor for corruption in India. It created a small controversy at the ANU among some postgraduate Indian students living in University House.

I wrote three poems sitting on the barsati. The first was 'Loving' for Tomi. Amrita – Tomi, as we fondly called her – got married in a temple, the kind of affair one now sees in several Bollywood films: the girl-boy fall in love; conservative parents don't want them to get married, different caste, religion, status, et cetera, et cetera. Tomi's boyfriend was a physicist from St Stephens College. He pursued her with Hindu passion, turmeric in complexion. Ivy wanted her youngest to marry a saved

Christian boy. A couple of meetings with churchgoing characters had ended in hilarious disasters. Anup managed to persuade Tomi to marry him. They have two lovely girls, Malika and Mishu. So one morning as we were visiting Ivy's home, I penned this piece.

Loving
for Tomi

Why should a rose
Bleed itself through its thorns?
Or a bird feel sad
When there's the whole sky
To sing and fly?

Each kiss, every touch
Is sometimes too little
Sometimes too much.

That's life, love,
They say.

But who' been a rose
Or knows
How close
A thorn is to its breast?

Or a bird which sings
Of love and madness
On each of its tiny wings?

Never having felt a bird's breath
Nor held a rose in heart's embrace
Or known grace on love's cruel face:
To live, we alone need each other's death.

My fellow writer from Fiji, the late Raymond Pillai, thought it was the most perfect poem I had composed.

Tomi and Anup by now occupied Ivy's ground floor; and it was always a pleasure to see them living so close to Ivy. It consoled our distant souls that Ivy was near her daughter and son-in-law in the same house and with two granddaughters. But closeness of one kind can create invisible distance of another kind.

*

Meanwhile, Anupa had married Philip Jacob, who found a manager's position in Doom Dooma tea estate in the jungles of Assam. In 1972, while returning from England to Fiji, after my studies there for two years, I flew from Delhi via Calcutta to be with them for a fortnight. Jyoti and our three children stayed with Ivy. It was an experience to remember.

The system was akin to indenture, with Philip, a very young man, with the status of a coolumber. He used to get up around four a.m., go to the tea estates and return to his spacious bungalow around eight a.m. for breakfast on the veranda surrounded by a beautifully spruced garden and rich vegetation. There must have been half a dozen servants looking after almost every need of Philip and Anupa.

Your shoes were polished early morning and kept in a neat line; breakfast cooked and laid on an elegant table; bathroom ready for your bath. I experienced a fortnight of most luxurious living but failed to see the lethal loneliness that my sister-in-law was suffering. It finally took its tragic toll.

*

The managerial positions on the tea estates were well-paid and much sought-after jobs with many perks for the men. The wives one met appeared complacent in their lonely idleness: only their club life was in full swing during the weekends. Many couldn't adjust to this life.

Anupa, with lively and curious mind, became increasingly isolated and drifted away from more than the place.

After a few years in that remote region, where you saw lit cities in the densest jungles, they returned to Ivy's house and lived with their three children for many months. A fourth child too was born there.

One night around midnight, Anupa in her desperation took some medication and never woke up fully. For four years, she was in a coma and finally died. I never saw her in that state; nor did I understand her inner grief and desolation of the spirit of the very spritely girl I'd known. She was a first-class student too.

But boughs break and hearts are torn asunder in the acts of living. And loving. While we were busy in the little things of life, she, a most lovely woman, lay dying.

This was the most traumatic event in Ivy's house. Ivy had lost her husband when he was in his forties; now a young daughter in her thirties. I cannot even imagine a mother's sorrow, seeing daily her child in that state in the bedroom next to hers. When we heard the news in Fiji, Jyoti immediately flew to Delhi to be with her mother and sister. When she returned almost a month later, Anupa's tragedy had taken its toll on my beautiful wife. Her father had died when she was very young; her mother had given Jyoti immeasurable love. And virtually every Christmas we went to Delhi to be with Ivy. No matter where we travelled, we always rerouted our trip via Delhi to spend a few days with Ivy in her most loving home. But this tragedy had cut to the bone and I do not think we ever fully recovered from its multiple effects. Jyoti was wounded as only a sister is by the death of her younger sibling.

Anupa was a schoolgirl when I came to know her – she was a prefect of her senior class and perfect scholar, always at the top of her class: every morning homework done, elegantly dressed, ready to catch the early bus to school. Clean and neat: her favourite line was, 'Chal hat makhi tu bari gandi hai!' The news of her comatose state, her suffering and finally mercifully her death, made me write a poem remembering and imagining her life and the sorrow she left behind in our hearts: I felt that of all her sisters, Aruna, every time she visited her mother, must have felt the daily pain of a sister dying in her mother's house, so the poem was dedicated to Aruna.

Anupam
for Aruna

The telegram was brief –

Just a sentence: simple but infinite
Time was precise, feelingless,
On an ordinary piece of paper
Dropped in my pigeon hole
As if from the beak of a bird
Meant for its nest
Or from the unsteady hand of a school girl :
Like you writing your first love letter.

The collision was complete
The fall: fatal, final.
It was all over-in the end
In fact a sense of relief.

Yet a comet-like grief
Hurtled in the spaces of my heart –
I stretched my thoughts to touch you
For one last time:
Like the rays of Delhi's winter sun –
Shimmering trees in Motibagh
I never cared to know their names
But suddenly, so important,
Through uncurtained windows
Playing on your eyelids
Closed in youthful bliss

I recall and remember
Your pure face like a morning glory
Opening up to the dawn.
Then smartly dressed for Jesus and Mary
In a red cardigan
An immaculate, virginal frock
The tiffin box tucked away
In a neat little bag:
A schoolgirl to perfection.

Life is such a terrible accident.

It's been drizzling since yesterday's dusk
The trees droop in drops
As if dressed for a funeral.
Who could have imagined such a dying?

You grew up dancing to life
I watched you play and laugh
The summer heat blew
Obsessive like a lover's breath
The parched earth parted
Till monsoons washed the flowers
You had put in your hair
After an evening in Moti Mahal
And then discarded them
On the steps of Sheila.
Such were the joys of a girl
Beautiful and beloved.

One evening a long-distance call
From the granite crags of mother's heart
Across waves of the seven seas

The news came thundering:
We were distraught for days, nights.
I couldn't write a word of comfort
Moments expanded into eternity
As between life and death.
Then silence: yours and ours.
While you were comatose
The world whirled and changed
The dust storms of Delhi
Often filled my eyes
The monsoon poured from my spirit
As rose petals lay lifeless
Around your hospital bed.

They wrote: you were out of pain
Alive, well-looked after-
A miracle was possible.
Daily we read Mummy's Bible
And whispered, prayed, betrayed.
Only you were so intensely indifferent
Like one close to the bone of truth.
I've walked amongst the ruins
Holding the hands of an ageing mother
Whose heart cried to one God,
Why? Why? Why? Why? Why?
The godless sky made no reply.
She prayed alone, we prayed together.
Others wept, slept,
To awake at midnight
To feel your pulse
To see if those lips stirred.
But nothing in nothing moved
Neither god nor your lips

Only faint heartbeats
Filling useless blood
Into drying arteries, dying cells.

We began waiting for the news
Irrevocable in plain words.
The telegram like a wreath
Brought back our breath
We knew the certain fate
As none of us knew you.

There's in this living city
A grave.
I'd dreamed of peacocks in the garden
Flowers in moonlight
Birds on trees, children on rocks
Women radiant with loveliness
Strolling on the edges of decay.
But you stood in my mind
Like some window in a church
Lit by rays of a setting sun
Among the twilight ruins
In despair, aware of another dawn.

I've visited it as a loved person or place
A garden where one swung from horizon to horizon
Over evenings as warm as cups of tea.

Then you crumbled:
A life so full, so precious.
All our strength and faith
Could not heal you
Nor all our prayers could reach you

As autumn leaves lay strewn
Like memories
In the withered grass of Motibagh.
Among the stark, wizened trees
Motionless is the swing
The window is draped in darkness
And no rays reach your little bed.

But beloved one
You leave behind more than a life.
You'll live in love
With remembered grace
And grief will not break a heart.
The sparrow will build its nest
Even with discarded telegrams
Written on common paper
White as the sheet that wrapped you
While they wept gently
For the loss of innocence with time.

Oh, Anupa
So much you gave to all of us;
So much taken by a single act
To the silence of a single grave.
O Anupam.

*

Anupa had four children. Philip turned out to be one caught in his own misery, haunted by his own demons. I never saw Anupa once she was comatosed. Anupa's death was the saddest, unspeakable episode in that home. They had returned from the tea estate and it wasn't a happy homecoming. Life and the visceral loneliness of marriage had made a beautiful woman break her vows and led to her death after the birth of her fourth child. Anupa needed help but no one was there to emotionally take care of her. Tragedy followed and the house was shadowed by a deepening sense of sorrow. But we didn't quite understand how she was dying inside. Until she was dead.

Ivy kept praying, and her faith gave us hope. Anupa's children grew into loving human beings – Kochu, Amitabh, Bui Aparna. Now they've families of their own, except Runi.

Anupa, their mother, died at thirty-eight.

*

As long as Ivy was there, we'd the centre of our lives and love in Delhi. Like birds, we built our nests on the Ivy tree by coming and going. Ivy's home was a sheltering tree, and stray birds had made their nests in its evergreen branches. They found shade and sustenance there. Ivy supported a network of missionary activities beyond Delhi and often joined the missionaries to go out for days preaching and living most frugally. She had a deep evangelical zeal in her soul but she was profoundly human too. That is what made her so extraordinary as a mother: thanks to the human heart by which we live, its tenderness, joys and fears – that was her gift to us all. She was always a mother first.

In front of the entrance to the building was a large tree, precariously growing on the eroding bank of the nallah. It was wired with an entwining vine of electric wires that carried light-giving electricity to the whole street. And telephone connections were wrapped round the branches and bole of the neem tree like the poor watchman in his winter clothes, leaning towards a wall.

A wiry bougainvillea grew and embraced the concrete pole connecting the wires of electricity and telephones. The red flowers appeared like drops of blood one sometimes saw on the pavements of streets in Delhi. Looking at this contraption, you marvelled how anything worked. But they did. When the electricity failed, you could hear the greying men in their grey clothes just outside on the street, growling at their 'sarvants'.

On it sometimes we saw a richly coloured kingfisher – a lone bird. Where he came from and vanished to we'd no idea but somehow it was a good omen for some members of the family. In an area where few birds flew, we kept a watch for the kingfisher in the debris of the nallah, where pigs ferreted for food and crows rode on pigs' black, muddy backs. It became a metaphor for me of corruption and I put the image in my poem 'Hope in Delhi'. It begins with these lines:

> The winter in Delhi
> Is warmed
> By a peanut-seller's angithi:
> The breath of Jamuna
> Blows cold, even now not unkind:
> Motes of dust glisten in the sun
> Then settle on the shrivelled skins
> Of men on stones,
> Of buffaloes warming against trees;
> While a crow rides on a pig's back
> Flapping its venal wings
> By a scavenger's demolished shack.
>
> The ruins of emperors
> Bleached by the summer's heat.
> Are silent wraiths
> Wrapped like coolies
> In an ominous decay;
> The phallic Kutub,
> Cowled near a detrited tomb,
> Stoops diminished in a distant gaze.
>
> Delhi like death has many faces.

Still, a city's dying monuments
Speak of life, as in winter
Spring comes back to mind…

This was written during the Indira Gandhi emergency – one ugly feature of this terrible blot on Indian democracy was the demolition of shacks from Delhi's environs where the poor dwelt; another was forced sterilisation by Sanjay Gandhi's ruthless brigade. In a college where my late friend Ramesh Rao taught, a dozen staff were detained for opposing the emergency. It was a shameful episode in modern India's inspiring epic of the freedom struggle.

*

Anup, with a postgraduate degree in physics from St Stephen's College, was a successful media and communications executive, president of a major advertising corporation. But his college friends were all overseas and he too wanted to go abroad for a change. He applied for a few jobs and was offered a lucrative position in a Middle East firm. Medical examination was part of the deal. He went through it all but there was terrible news: he'd terminal lung cancer. He'd smoked for thirty-five years from his college days at St Stephen's. He was given six months to live. The despair in the family was palpable. Malika and Amrita went everywhere to seek some cure for this incurable malady – the pitiless emperor of all maladies.

Anup survived for almost eight years. He wrote two remarkable books. The first, *The Joy of Cancer*, launched by actor Sunil Dutt, became an overnight bestseller. A new lease of life had begun for Anup and he was a speaker at many places to many people out of which came his second book – stories of many cancer patients in many corners of India. I felt he had regained his lust for life and was working resuming his profession in Delhi.

He wrote, 'It was ironical that in the face of death, I began, for the first time, to really live.'

Anup had many college friends and it is with him that I met a few of my former Doscos, now managing big firms and senior public servants, ambassadors and whatnot. He was also fond of our children and took them to see festivals and places I'd not seen. I think he'd a deeper sense of place than most of us. He was keen that we saw aspects of ancient India, away from Delhi. Married to a Christian, he possessed a genuine Hindu sensibility.

One evening, Anup rang us to say Pansy Aunty had died. Pansy, Ivy's older and beautiful sister, had no children. She never lost her girlish ways or values and she was our children's easy Aunty Pansy who played cards and carom and Chinese checkers and celebrated Christmas with little gifts for everyone.

Age had undone so many and Pansy was next on the list. Pansy was ninety-five when we got the message that she had died in her sleep. She was a tall, attractive Rajasthani woman but married a drunkard. Life had become a nightmare. She'd been an education inspector in Rajasthan but in her retirement she came and stayed with Ivy in her house. It was moving to see the care of a younger sister for her older one – one who had a much easier life than Ivy.

One night while Pansy was in deep sleep, Ivy made me come to her room and look at the sleeping face of her sister. I was moved by the sight but more by the act of Ivy, for she was, I think, giving me some intimations of old age and its utter helplessness in the desolation of sleep, the premonitions of mortality.

*

In Fiji one evening as Jyoti and I were going out to dinner with a few friends, the news came through Ajay Singh, the then Indian high commissioner in Suva, that Anup had collapsed in the bathroom and died. Shock and sorrow overwhelmed my heart. He was fifty-eight and my two children's favourite uncle. He took them to Puskar Fair in Rajasthan and many other places for them to see on the Indian trains – one of his brothers was the chief of Northern Railways. I also went with him, Tomi, Malika and Mishu for ten days to Corbett Park in the foothills of the Himalayas. He wanted to show us some wildlife of India and the majestic beauty of the mountains, rivers and forests, lit by the burning eyes of wild tigers and flying peacocks.

Anup had time for us. Suddenly he was no more.

In his memory, I wrote a poem:

So?

My distant heart, so mildewed with grief
In a wet season, a single dry leaf.
Who could have across the seas foretold
So soon the body will grow so icy cold.
All I've is a house, an absence of breath:
Full of friends, mourning a death.

The man is gone, untouched by my hand
A passing stranger in a houseless land.

The deeps of a heart, the depths of an ocean
Could not hold a singular life's devotion
Imagine now the sorrows, the tears of a face
Nothing will fill so large, so empty a space.

He was my brother: in my remembering heart
His presence is there, though worlds apart;
He may live in words, in tear-dimmed dreams
Pebbles of memory rolling in so many streams.

In my mildewed soul, a silent grief
It knows: life can be so fatal, so brief.
All I need is some small unbroken part
Holding on: breaking my beating heart.

A-1/177 had more visitors than any house in the neighbourhood. Even the taxi stand knew. The moment you rang, '*Achaji Mummy ke ghar par. Abhi ayaa!*' came the voice of a sardarji whose tribe seemed to own all the taxis in Delhi through their hard work and business acumen. Ivy's house gave them the most business because of many international visitors throughout the year. The visitors never haggled for the fare either, for by foreign standards, the taxi fare in Delhi was cheap beyond belief.

Our daughter Kavita was born four years after the house was built. Jyoti came to Delhi from Fiji for the birth of our last child. Kavita was a few months old when one lunchtime she choked on her mother's milk. In panic, Jyoti ran downstairs with the baby. Below lived a colonel and he immediately got into his car and drove the mother and the child to the nearest hospital. One look at the baby, who had grown blue like baby Krishna, had convinced the colonel that this was an emergency. As soon as they reached the hospital, the baby revived and the doctors and the nurses thanked the condition of the Delhi roads for saving our child's life. The undulating surface of the road had made the milk flow out of her windpipe and the choking had ceased.

I do not know where the colonel is today. But when Jyoti arrived at Nausori airport after almost six months in Delhi and told this grim story with a happy ending, I felt grateful to see our baby and the mother in her green sari descending the gangway of Air Pacific at Nausori airport. The joy of seeing my wife with our little girl made up for the tragedy that almost happened.

So many times I feel we've been saved from death by God's grace and Ivy's prayers. We're all mortal but someone's love can make us feel immortal.

Once again, a tragedy almost happened: one holiday our son Rohan was in Delhi with the family. I was still in Suva. As I landed at Indira Gandhi airport at Palam, I was told how close Rohan came to a tragedy by an overdose of bhang mixed in Holi drinks celebrated in Delhi with noisy and colourful passion. One of Rohan's cousins had mixed a lot of bhang in the drinks being consumed by their college mates. Rohan had no idea and kept drinking it like Australian beer. Soon he was in the throes of intense pain and he was rushed to the hospital nearby.

'Luckily,' said the doctor, 'you've brought him in time, otherwise it could have been fatal.'

Jyoti remembers Rohan's face and words. Tomi and Anup understood how close Rohan had been to a tragedy. Luckily, Jyoti was there and a mother's instinct saved our son's life. And how Aunt Amrita kept awake that night.

*

Jyoti had arrived back in July; in August, we were on our way to England on a Commonwealth fellowship for two years: the family of five, via Delhi. Ivy came to London and we spent a summer there with Amrita, who was working for Air India. We rented a place and that was our happiest holiday in England. Ivy returned home to Delhi. Amrita used to visit us in Leeds with duty-free bottles of a variety of liquor. And when we left our rented flat in Leeds, my university friends carried several bottles each on the night of our farewell.

Sadly, I lost touch with my friends at Leeds, the university that opened a whole new world through Commonwealth literature for me. V.S. Naipaul and Patrick White became my favourite authors.

*

After the completion of my second Masters, we were back in Delhi. Rohan and Gita loved their Nani's home. They were taken on evening 'walks' by the two ayahs in the empty space in front of the house. The rugged path through the empty park glimmered and gleamed in the after-rain sunshine like pather panchali and we walked often on it to call a scooter to Connaught Place. An occasional cow or buffalo would be seen grazing on the rubbishladen opposite bank of the nallah. But we got used to it and nobody noticed the koora-karkat thrown in the nallah by the civil servants staying in their government quarters, crudely constructed and archaic buildings overloaded with concrete.

To have government quarters was a real privilege in Delhi for these government employees from many parts of India. Many sent their children to Ivy's schools. Their civic sense was caste-ridden – someone from the lower caste should clean their unholy garbage: it was sanctioned by the holy scriptures. Or was it? You saw young bureaucrats walking with ash caste marks or a red mark on the centre of their oily forehead, hair dyed jet-black.

On weekends, schoolchildren played cricket in that open ground with great gusto and I watched them with interest from Ivy's balcony. Mule Ram, one of Ivy's cooks, who was a double of Michael Somare in looks, was our favourite chef in the house.

He worked for Ivy for years and made the most delicious dishes of Indian curries and Western desserts. The kitchen was connected to the dining room but we seldom entered it – it was the cook's exclusive domain and he cooked the most delectable meals for a large family with very basic utensils and a few modern gadgets. Ivy's kitchen was quite small and in summer heat it must have been unbearable. It was a colony compared to the rest of the house, large and spacious as an empire.

Then one fine day, we heard Mule Ram had found a job in a government department. We were all happy for him – a government of India job for a cook was progress of a high order. He was replaced by Lala, his assistant, again a hard-working cook but also quite a crook. Ivy had no time for counting her money, and all and sundry took full advantage of her openness and generosity, including her box of jewels.

She supported many pastors in the northern parts of Delhi and Punjab and when the missionaries came, she joined them with her van and driver. The new brown Maruti was driven by Samson – a small, baldish, wiry fellow. He was an excellent driver and knew Delhi streets like the lines on the palm of his hand. Delhi traffic is another universe of colliding galaxies – I tried to drive a car in Delhi once and caused an accident after a few kilometres. Samson took us all over the place, morning, noon and midnight. He lived on the barsati in a rather large room on weekends joined by his mysterious wife and son. We hardly saw them. But I often saw Samson smiling at the neighbour's housemaid. From the barsati, he had a good view of the world, both in the neighbours' kitchens and the ganda nallah.

Samson was a Christian in name only, I think. He read the newspapers every morning and told you the grimmest news of the national capital. But he was intimately familiar with roads, margs, streets, galis of Delhi and drove the brown Maruti with some pride. We could take him anywhere and he would find the place. He was, I think, genuinely fond of Ivy. Jyoti and I appreciated that quality in him. He was most interested in taking foreign visitors to any part of Delhi and beyond.

Muriel Aunty and Pansy Aunty were his companions to church gatherings and prayers. Like a good Christian, he'd listen to them and showed them the respect due to his elders. Ivy trusted him implicitly. The brown van was his, though owned by Mummy.

Ivy had lost her husband when she was barely forty-two. And there were five young girls. But her fortitude and foresight made her a remarkable educationist – occasionally her annual school concerts were attended by Chacha Nehru, the PM. Nehru's birthday in India is celebrated as Children's Day.

*

Anupa, then Pansy Aunty and finally Anup died in that house. And as long as Ivy was a presence there, Jyoti and I visited Delhi virtually every Christmas. Often with our three children. Kavita our youngest was closest to her grandmother. We named her Kavita Ivy.

But it was Ivy who was the spiritual heart of her house. While I loved visiting Delhi, it was when leaving Ivy around midnight to catch a flight to Singapore or Bangkok or KL that I often felt my heart would split with sorrow at leaving such a loving mother. Living in that house, where I felt most at home, I wrote a few poems to see into the life of this extraordinary woman in her eighties growing old. I now feel I never quite understood the sorrows of her heart, nor the deepening faith with which she'd sheltered us whenever some tragedy hit our lives illness, death, coups, migration.

For me, she became the symbol of Mother India.

With those ruins glinting in the Delhi's winter sunset:

Ruins

I've walked amongst ruins
Where the princess dreamt of love
With her betel-red lips
And her lover's mark hidden
Across her bosom
By a silken shawl –
A mere smudge
Seen as the crescent moon
Through trees in prayer.

I've heard the silence in the grass
Singing the splendour of the past
As squirrels scampered across
Blood-red roses, jasmines white
To see the peacock dance
In its courtly magnificence.

I've felt in my heart
The pain of the dead
And understood the restless heart
Like a wave on the ocean's bosom
Longing to hug the shore.
Such betrayal, such love
In so many ruins.

In my natal land
There are no such ruins
Except in the arteries of the old;
But in the country of the mind
They are faceless, eyeless.

Here there are no palaces
Here no peacocks dance
Under the dark clouds
So full of dreams
A princess by the window.

It takes generations
They say
To create even ruins.

*

There were times when I was so moved by Ivy's daily life that I began capturing it in my poems, even as my imagination faltered at the reality of growing old. Ivy lived on the first floor. She'd to climb twenty white marbled steps to reach her drawing room, washed clean, zharaed-pochoed, by a woman who came every morning and wiped the whole house of dust, but I always felt she left it dirtier than before! Ivy would climb the steps slowly but by herself.

Steps

Washed, polished, there they are:
The steps – slightly chipped, scarred:
Eighteen or twenty
For reasons I cannot explain
Was it ignorance or pain?
I never counted them exactly.

A shadow moves across my heart:
Step by step
She climbed them
Almost daily.
This clean steady concrete
Below her bone-bare feet
A tide-like heaving
More substantial than any memory.

Other 'Steps' in a painting
Hang in the dim light
In the grey corner, with a green door
Shimmering as her beautiful hair.

You cannot miss a step on the stairs
Rung by rung, we grew;
Nests on a tree
Spiralling into other worlds.

But where's that sparrow of my sorrow?
Seen through the window pane.
The nest is empty
The boughs grieve
The leaves mourn
Their loss so fruitfully.

But I remember
A mother's Alzheimer's
And how she held on to the balustrade
The other hand clutching a stranger's?
It did not matter:
Memory had lost its grip.
Hand by hand she climbed
Towards a starless sky.

In the soft rain falling
She never faltered or fell
Nor in summer's harsh light
Or winter's half night.
For long after, in distant laughter,
She'd no reason to remember
A season of desolation
When flowers on graves die.

The solid steps are there
They creep over us
In our heart's silence;
No footfalls are heard
Only in the footprints of her faith
An invisible radiance
Touched by our breath.

We hold her life
In an indelible prayer
Like the daily bread.

Then, suddenly,
We miss a step, a heartbeat,
And fall among her stars.

*

The house that Ivy built almost fifty years ago was to be demolished. Jyoti, Anupa's children and her other sisters sold the upper floors of the house and the one school she had maintained in her old age. Amrita kept hers – the ground floor. There's a whole history in the rooms, walls, cupboards and steps of the house. For me, it is the great house of memories. Its poignancy is more deeply felt when you remember that Ivy slowly but surely was losing her memory. Often she didn't recall the faces of her daughters. This broke my Jyoti's heart.

The tears and joys of things and voices will be heard no more. That woman Shanti who malished Ivy won't come there any more; nor the preachers and teachers: Mummy's many friends like Pastor George. We sometimes made quiet fun of their prayer meetings and hymn singing but never quite understood the deep roots of their faith: Ivy was the rock on which more than a church stood throughout our stormy nights, from Fiji to Delhi.

Our children, with their many cousins, won't be running around with a sense of abandon that their Nani's home gave them.

Gitanjali was posted as a diplomat in Delhi for three years but her Nani had gone by then. With her sense of the spiritual, Gita would have understood her grandmother with deeper love and understanding. That it never happened is the greater loss. Because Ivy had died, we didn't visit Gita in Delhi even once.

*

But I do remember how, wrapped in her pink-coloured gown, Mummy used to make tea early in the morning for us, Jyoti and me.

Morning Tea

Morning's grey face, wrinkled,
A dishevelled mother's.
The joints entwined
Creak in a rusted bed
Of a body knotted in bones.
The indignities of age
Wearing of socks, teeth,
And a torn shawl, a gown,
The shuffle of chappals
The muteness of our mortal coil
Unwinding without resistance or rage.

A light switch clicks
No brightness falls
Even from the dirty moon
Idling o'er a dark city.

Outside the fog gloats
Cloaks trees, houses,
And the corrupting sludge
Of an open drain
Suppurating like an old omen.
There's no sign of rain.

I turn to sleep:
It'll be a long day
Of stray thoughts
Circling like crows
In a dhobi's unwashed sky.

Lives have gone
Only a day like a sad song
Now seems so long
A requiem without a raga.

This long and daily journey
One step at a time to the kitchen
This assault on the summit
Is it the sum of us all?

The tap drips filling my mind
With island memories
Of a boat on dry sands.
The clock ticks
Waves lap the shore:

A knock on the door
My wake-up call
A light enters from a burnt-out candle.
She's handing a cup of tea
With her gentle trembling hand
Almost ninety.

Fingers with broken nails
Cling stubbornly to the chipped plate

Fate's final lila
Ah, Queen Lear.

Suddenly a mote in the rising sun
Shone with immortality.

*

When Ivy died, Jyoti was with her. Neither my three children nor I were able to attend her funeral. This great grief has remained buried deep in my heart. Jyoti perhaps understood it and when we visited Delhi a year later, she held a memorial service for her mother. It was also to make us feel better that we'd participated in a ceremony of farewell for someone who had loved us unconditionally. Now we visit her grave in the churchyard where she's buried next to her husband. Not far from the parents' grave is Anupa's, with a few red roses in the shadows of a large tree.

When I heard the news of Ivy's death, I was with my children and grandchildren at Rohan's house for a barbecue lunch. The heart-rending news of Ivy's dying was suddenly beyond us – we left the lunch and went home. In the evening, I went for a walk. The hills shone in the setting sun and on the horizons trees appeared like passing caravans.

Sitting on a wooden bench, I wrote 'Ivy':

Mummy is dead. A mother is gone. Nani is no more.

You never know the depth of your love for someone until you cannot touch her.

Your world loses its balance: you cannot imagine the absences. And how we love best what we've lost forever.

Rarely the dying of a single tree diminishes a whole orchard.

We'd all built our nests on her boughs. She was always there: her gift of love was her deepest gift.

Imagine Mummy's room: its empty desolation, its unspeakable silence. Only the sparrows flitting in and out of the windows and the dripping of the taps. That steel cupboard, her one tin trunk, the iron bed. Her grey cloth-covered much read and red-marked Bible. And that cross hanging on the bare yellow wall. The simple calendar proclaiming, The Lord is my Shepherd…

This dark sobbing in my heart will not cease. A whole world has suddenly vanished. I never knew a broken leaf could contain so much grief. And who will climb those stairs, step by step, slowly with so much strength of will. Who will give us faith to bear our sorrows or prayers to live by?

For two months, with Jyoti, I'd seen the details of her life and dying revealed in the lethal dailiness of care and love. It was a privilege no matter how heartbreaking.

Canberra is sunburnt this Christmas and drought-stricken. The water is running low. But a few roses bloom in my garden in the new house. Hannah Maya loves feeling them, petal soft as her great granma's cheeks almost like hers. I wish we could send with Hannah a few rosebuds to Delhi to be placed on the mute radiance of Ivy's grave.

Not far from our home in Gungahlin is a lake. Little beyond is a hillock with a single wooden bench. Often I sit on it and watch the sunset: how dark clouds are lit by the sun's golden light. It is infinitely beautiful to behold this exquisite splendor of the dying light. Its magic and mystery. So much loveliness in the passing of light over a landscape.

For some reason then I remember Ivy and think: shall not her loveliness be loved forever?

But who cares about roses when a whole orchard is gone.

*

Last year in July, Jyoti and I visited the house and had a lunch with Tomi. The trees and flowers were blooming after the monsoonal rains. Delhi can look very green, washed of dust and dirt and visible pollution. The ancient ruins are camouflaged by tall, leafy trees. Monsoon saves the city in myriad ways. The nallah is being filled with brown soil and black rocks. Soon there will be more houses, government apartments perhaps, and Amrita thinks there will be a park too, in a small corner. The open ground in front of Ivy's house has been filled with hurriedly erected structures. The park, like part of one's lung, has disappeared, amputated.

The area looks overcrowded and a few tall buildings have come up and the narrow street from Zhandu Singh Marg is overcrowded with bigger cars. Sandhills abound as contractors build multi-storeyed houses in place of old ones. At night, it's difficult to know where to turn into Ivy lane to reach Ivy Home. We've lost more than an open park, an identity of a place so loved and lived.

But the house that Ivy built will remain in my memory like a sunflower in sarso fields I'd seen in the villages from which my grandparents had migrated to Fiji, 135 years ago this May. I'd gone to these villages with Saeed's very poetic brother Shanne. Travelling in a hired van in the villages of UP, near Lucknow, I was thinking of Ivy's house, for it had in a sense given me the lost world of my grandparents. I'd found a home of love and generosity long after they had lost their mulk.

*

Once when I was alone in that house, I missed Jyoti deeply. She was teaching in Canberra and I was attending a conference. I wrote 'Absences' one afternoon when everyone had gone to church.

Absences
for Jyoti

Writing about the dead
Is easy. History has its beginnings
Sometimes even an end.
Roots like cables lie
Entangled across wild seas, old griefs.

Words, I'd imagined, could become
Companions to their solitude.

Sorry is sometimes too much.

This room, ample, bare
With a naked bulb, two half-burnt candles
A dim light warms the wall.
Sparrows flit by the window in a winter haze
The mirror is rust-covered
Like a line of the Bhagwad Gita.

I cannot see my face in that mirror
Water leaks into the cracked sink.
A few books lined on a wooden table
By the illiterate woman
Who grins and sweeps
Dust at every dawn.
Ivy is gone her absence
Is the real presence.
I'm, I must confess, unable
To write the sorrows
Of generations' servitude.

The birds, like children,
Fly over houses and hills
On and on to their islands of exile.

I think of two deaths
On this heavy, timbered bed
Where once voices sang hymns
Where now I lie
Tears shaking my heart.

The ceiling fan revolves
Like a wounded bird.

I can neither sleep nor weep
For the past
Nor hold in my hands
The present pain.
Between me and the sparrows
There's just the window pane.
Outside the chowkidaar sleeps
Curled in his tiny space.
The ghosts have slipped into the house
Through crevices in my memory:
They nibble and gnaw
My heart's sinews.
While rain patters on the barsati
Stirring blue islands on a barsaat ki raat.

I miss you:
This winter you sang in me a while
Filling the emptiness of more than a room;
Against your bones, I'd felt,
A song deeper than I'd known before.

*

Ivy's greatest gift to me was her love and Jyoti. She was closest to her second daughter and for her she travelled to Fiji three times, England once, and finally to Australia with her friend Sister Lal, who looked after her and made hot, fresh chapattis even in Canberra. Jyoti and I spent almost all our Christmases in Delhi and every trip we made abroad for study or conferences, our route was always via New Delhi. I think we were lucky to spend so many holidays with Ivy. Her home at A-1/177 Safdurjung Enclave was our home.

Now that she's no more, Delhi for me has lost much of its human attraction as if the centre is no more, although two of my dear sisters-in-law still live there. Delhi is the home of Aruna and Amrita. Almost all their lives they have lived in Delhi. Only Amrita has really lived on the ground floor of Ivy's house. The other two levels now belong to two Delhi families who have purchased the property. That is why now the old house is being demolished and a new, bigger building is being contemplated, if not actually constructed. Amrita will have a more spacious home on the ground floor. That nallah is being filled for a park and perhaps a few more buildings in a very crowded part of the city called Delhi.

Ivy's beautiful home will be no more her children's pilikothi – the magnificent residence in Nasirabad, where Ivy and her sisters had grown up, was also lost to strangers. Only Amrita had shown some interest in her mother's past and visited the places where she'd played as a child with herons walking on the withered sedge by the lake.

But houses rise and fall. Men and women break like boughs. And we migrate like exiles on the surface of our world, searching for some sense of permanence. In vain – perhaps that is our vanity trying to escape mortality.

It was while I was a student that I compiled a collection of pictures and writings for an assignment as a teacher in training. It made a colourful album of poetry, prose, and pictures of scenes, houses, birds, flowers and faces. On one page was a picture, on the facing page a piece of writing to go with the picture. Perhaps that later influenced me to title my first slender volume of poems *Faces in a Village*. Writing for me may have begun with that exercise of other people's written words.

Anupa was doing her Senior Cambridge examination and when she passed it in the first grade, I gave the picture book to her as a gift.

*

How often I think of Ivy who gave me gifts beyond measure, not only in her daughter Jyoti but a whole family and a home in Delhi. Two years ago, before she passed away in A-1/177, Jyoti was with her for three months. We should have stayed longer with Ivy – given a few years of our lives to be with her. She was an independent woman, widowed in her early forties but for the next almost fifty years no one I've known has had deeper self-respect, independence of mind and a radiant faith in her Christ. Her children turned out to be no more than nominal Christians. Her five daughters married men of different faiths: two Hindus, one Muslim, two Syrian Christians. She was an orchard for her grandchildren.

We named Kavita after Ivy. Gita's middle name is Jyoti and Rohan's is Fazal, Jyoti's dad's name.

One cannot conquer grief but one can survive and transcend it through memories of love and human touch. By loving others.

Often in the heat of Delhi, I used to get severe headaches. In the middle of the night, Ivy used to tiptoe to our room, pray for me and touch my head so gently that I felt healed and happy. 'Sleep,' she'd whisper and wake us to have tea with her in her room while a gentle, healing rain fell, flooding the open drain.

The touch of that vanished hand only now I'm beginning to understand. And the silence of a mother's beloved voice. There are things that haunt you forever; there are remembrances that can harrow your heart; there are also individuals who hallow your lives.

I've known Jyoti now for more than fifty years – nothing has changed except that love becomes stronger and once you've known it, nothing can destroy it. Loving you eternally with a love that's true: from the start within my heart it seems I've always known the sun would shine when you're mine....

4. Return Flight to Paradise

A Small Country

Did I confuse the categories?
Was I blind?
Was I afraid of hubris
in identifying this land
with the kingdom? Those stories
about the far journeys, when it was here
at my door; the object
of my contempt that became
the toad with the jewel in its head!
Was a population so small
enough to be called, too many
to be chosen? I called it
an old man, ignoring the April
message proclaiming: Behold,
I make all things new.

The dinosaurs have gone their way
into the dark. The time-span
of their human counterparts
is shortened; everything
on this shrinking planet favours the survival
of the small people, whose horizons
are large only because they are content to look at them
from their own hills
I grow old,

> bending to enter the promised land that was here all the time,
> happy to eat the bread that was baked
> in the poets oven, breaking my speech
> from the perennial tree
> of my people and holding it in my blind hand.
>
> – R.S. Thomas

On 11 February 1993, I left Canberra on my way, via Sydney, to Nadi the place of my birth. It was exactly five years, two months and eight days when I'd left Nadi to come to Canberra. Five long, long years. But when I landed at Nadi airport, soon after midnight, I didn't hear the 'still, sad music of humanity': just the claptrap of tourists, stamping of visas, clanking of duty-free liquor (you're now allowed three litres, the shop notice proclaimed in garish colours) and the flaps and the weight of the baggage belt.

Paradise was in after-midnight darkness.

As I waited for my baggage (the belt snakes at snail's speed), my eyes were attracted to a rather large, touristic mural on the opposite wall; all the faces are of native Fijians giving a collective hibiscus smile. I was struck by the absence of a single Indian face on that grotesquely coloured piece of commercial art. Perhaps the Indians are lucky, I thought, not to be in that absurdity to be so crudely used and exposed.

I picked up my luggage and turned. Most of the customs officials and the taxi drivers were Indians. Outside, the air was fresh and there was a haze of light around the terminal buildings. Terminal! For a moment, I was stunned because the Qantas and tourist ads in Australia gave no idea of an Indian presence: a people who remain nameless, faceless, voiceless, landless and are slowly becoming countryless. They are the invisible people of Fiji – the outsiders within. Like blood in the body, seen only when cut. They bleed.

I had left Fiji in December 1987, after the two Fijian coups, with my wife and two children. I'd come to Canberra for a few months, where my son Rohan was studying, but I'd remained longer than I'd intended. This, my first visit since, I was undertaking alone. As I sat at Sydney's Kingsford Smith airport, I remembered that in Suva we'd named a park after that extraordinarily intrepid aviator.

*

Waiting for QF 17 at Sydney, I'd felt no particular emotion: neither excitement, nor dread, nor any expectations. Only deep down a sense of melancholy – not unlike what the eldest son feels when, after his father's cremation, the following morning he goes to collect his father's charred bones and a handful of ashes to enshrine the remains into the sea or a river. This ancient rite – from fire to water – gives grace and completeness to the dead so that the living can continue their life without ghosts.

Except that the past, like our parents, lives on in us.

That afternoon when I left Evatt in a taxi for Canberra airport, my mind was full of ghosts.

In the afternoon, the slanting light was bright and Tom, the taxi driver, was talkative. 'Have a chat!' he declared blithely and gave me a rundown of the impending Australian elections for the next twenty minutes. He was also a cricketer who had broken his left foot by simply stepping on a cricket ball. But, he said, he'd made a fortune betting on the West Indies in the current series. He thought I was from India and asked me how he felt about Border's imminent demolition of Sunil Gavaskar's test record.

I said I liked Alan Border immensely but most Indians would prefer Australia to be a country without borders! He didn't quite get the pun. He looked like a public servant, making an extra buck, but claimed he was illiterate. From my childhood in Fiji, I had assumed anyone who spoke English was literate, and those who didn't were illiterate.

At the Qantas check-in counter, I told a balding young man that I'd checked in at Canberra. He commented authoritatively, 'Canberra people do everything wrong,' and rechecked my booking and examined the boarding pass thoroughly before handing it back to me.

I passed through immigration, security check and duty-free shopping without a hassle even if I looked a bit like a Bedouin Arab.

*

It's six o'clock. I stroll to gate 30, from where QF 17 will take us into its belly like a whale and then take off like a magnificent bird that it is, a floating miniature Mother Earth. In the lounge, there's just a single person: a plump, darkish Indian woman dressed in a white blouse, white skirt, pink stockings and black shoes. She has a heavy look about her and reminds me of Josephine the girl-woman who looked after our domestic affairs just before the coups. Josephine, whenever she was fed up with the drudgery of domestic work, threatened to migrate to Australia.

Sydney airport is in a perpetual state of repair and refurbishment. The café inside is empty except for the plastic chairs; outside, the brutality of steel lay scattered on a hot tarmac. The image of guns flits across my mind as I see a few jumbos dozing like sharks. The remembrance of guns should have agitated me but my mind is as seemingly tranquil as the Pacific.

Josephine's double walks towards the cafeteria: her gait reminds me of my two sisters, big, bountiful village women. My younger sister's crippled husband had died in Auckland recently. His body was flown to Fiji for cremation: I hadn't attended the funeral, just as I hadn't attended Dr Timoci Bavadra's. So this journey was, in a sense, some atonement for neglected emotions. My brother-in-law, aged fifty-nine, was cremated at the Wailoaloa beach, next to the Denarau tourist centre, where my father's pyre had burnt almost fifteen years ago. My brother-in-law's pyre must have been lit at the same spot, under the rusting corrugated-iron shed. Another death, a different father, a different son, almost a different country.

And my indifference.

I sit down not far from 'Josephine'. She has two cabin bags, well stuffed, possibly full of gifts. She's carrying a large, plastic pink doll in a box. Around seven thirty p.m., we board the aircraft. It's less than half full: I feel pleased, the service will be better. I've a window seat. A few seats away to my left there's a Fijian couple with two lively children. The mother scolds them in Fijian; the father smiles at me indulgently. At exactly eight p.m. the plane taxies for take-off. The children become quiet, strapped to their seats. Outside, Sydney seems cool. In the soft glow, the city looks like a shawl of shimmering luminosity.

The flight time is three hours thirty minutes. 'Fasten seat belts, extinguish cigarettes, seats upright,' in dull, drill tones. Then the demonstration: I wonder if the life jackets really inflate in an emergency. They should show it by really pulling the tags and blowing the whistle. After all, they are flying over a vast stretch of the largest ocean in the world. A smiling hostess flashes by. The runway lights are now gleaming; the city lights blazing. Our aircraft is waiting to be airborne on a runway that shines like a steel blade of a cane knife.

As the plane takes off, tearing the silence, I take out a six-page English translation of a story of Totaram Sanadhaya entitled 'The Story of the Haunted Line'. The story is, in fact, an autobiographical fragment of an Indian's indentured life in the fetid lines (barracks) in a corner of Fiji. Nothing much survives of the thoughts, feelings, memories of the indentured Indians, the victims of this new system of slavery. The British had a genius for inventing games and systems for the subjugation of other people; if the game were full of rules, the atrocious systems of many oppressions were often legally done.

Fiji had the highest suicide rate of any colony at the close of the nineteenth century. So Totaram's piece is priceless like one or two surviving 'girmityas'. It's about exile and loneliness; suicide and survival; Fiji and India; and a telling encounter between the first migrant Indians and a handful of Fijians. A moving and rare narrative: perhaps a creative opening into one hundred years of servitude that remains unarticulated, buried like ancestral bones. But breaking the bread with the dead means giving those bones a life in lines of poetry. So here's the substance for a good poem, I think. Perhaps I can write it when I am in Fiji in my village. The idea pleases me for I have the title too: 'Lines Across Black Waters'.

I ask for a Bloody Mary as we swing towards the open sea. The city is silhouetted against a darkening sky. A few boats are bobbing below like a flock of ducks. There's the laughter of a baby as in the Huggies ad; as we soar, the harbour recedes with a last glimpse of the Opera House glinting like marbled lotus petals at the edge of a blue lake in the after-light of a burnt-out sun; yachts are moths floating as our aircraft circles and climbs above the clouds, fluffs of wool, towards Lord Howe Island. We are on our way to Nadi – name of a river, a village, a town, a district and now the international airport, two miles away from my home where some people worshipped Nandi, Shiva's bull of plenty. Shiva, the god of dance of life and death; Shiv, the first name of my dead father.

I order another Bloody Mary: Shiva the god and my father Shiv were both fond of 'nasha': liquor in their breath.

An American woman next to me says, 'There's a drink called Virgin Mary, you know.'

No, I didn't know. My initiation into the pleasures of wine had come through Bob Brissenden and Alec Hope, two civilised poets of Canberra.

She explained, 'It's without vodka.'

It's dark outside – 32C. We adjust our watches to Fiji time.

*

My trip to Fiji had been planned a few weeks ago. I was going to India, England and Europe on a reading, lecture and study tour for about three months. It occurred to me that I hadn't seen my eldest brother, my elder sister and my youngest brother and their family for more than five years. Then, my eldest brother and his wife were leaving for a visit to New Zealand, where more than fifty members of my family had migrated after the second Fijian coup. This was their first flight outside Fiji. So I hurried to Nadi, the place of my birth, where my father and his father's bones were burnt and their ashes buried in the waves of this most peaceful ocean. My mother still lived, aged almost eighty, on its shore.

As I ruminated, the wine trolley rolled by. 'Wine, sir?'

I nodded.

There were two choices: a cheap red and a cheaper white. Qantas could do better in its choice of Aussie wines. I declined and fished out the *Airways* magazine. In it, there was a piece called 'Call me Ismail' on Ismail Merchant, a key member of one of the world's most successful film-making trio, IvoryMerchant-Jhabvala. I had seen almost everything they had made, except *Howards End*.

'Call me Ismail' was a clever title, echoing the first line of Melville's classic *Moby Dick* set in the Pacific. 'Call me Ishmael' is a remarkable opening line of the novel. And the whale, a divine retribution. And some people never discover who Moby Dick is. The content of the article was disappointing except for one lovely portrait of Merchant with director James Ivory and writer Ruth Jhabvala. I put the magazine back and closed my eyes.

The lights are switched on: we are descending to land at Nadi airport in twenty-five minutes. Still no flutter in the heart, just a momentary worry whether they'd let me in. There was a time we couldn't leave Fiji without military sanction.

I walk straight to the immigration official, a young woman with a blue cap. The young don't remember old politicians. My passport is stamped.

A young Indian customs inspector whispers, 'Doc, just walk through.'

I do.

As I come out, the air is balmy: my youngest brother is there; and my eldest brother is there with his three married sons, sunflowers in the dark. We drive to my young brother's home behind Nadi town. We sit on the veranda and have cups of tea. It's two a.m. The little town of my childhood and youth is asleep; so is my mother. I shall see her at dawn.

*

During my week-long stay in Fiji, most evenings I spend in Maigania, the village where I was born, on the banks of the Nandi river. Across the river is a Fijian village, Molowai. The river was our meeting place: in its waters we swam, on its sands we sat building sandcastles, and played 'pakki' in what was known as Kalpu's kund. On the river's bank we played soccer, ate pawpaws, drank coconut water, boiled and roasted corn on the cob: there was such an abundance of food even in a flood.

Occasionally we fished, bathed cows and horses – and looked at village women, Indians and Fijians, washing heaps of dirty clothes in the ever flowing water. Sometimes in midday sun these women sat astride over fallen tree trunks, the water lapping their thighs like village men's passions. The men worked on the farms, harvested tonnes of cane, ate copiously and copulated with a sense of wanton abandon. *Voices in the River*, my collection of poems, was about life by the banks of this river, and perhaps a bit more.

It was about one such man that in 1988 I wrote my first short story published in a newspaper. When 'Bro's Funeral' appeared in the *Canberra Times*, it gave me immense delight. My first piece of creative writing after the coups and after I had left Fiji. Distance had sharpened my awareness of my lost childhood and boyhood and feeling for a stolen world. Bro was not my brother; he is, in fact, my brother's neighbour and friend, more than a dozen years older than my brother.

We called him kaka, father's younger brother. When Bro heard I was making my revenant visit to my brother's, he came to see me: washed, brushed, hair well-oiled and combed, dressed in a new pair of trousers and an immaculate white shirt: 'suited-booted', as my mother said. He was in amazingly good health, face shining with coconut oil with blotches of talcum powder.

Bro, a farmer on a ten-acre farm given to his mother by the CSR company after her girmit, had arranged the marriages of his eleven children. Then he himself had remarried after the death of his first wife. He spoke proudly of his achievements: his cane-cutting ability, his sexual prowess under increasingly difficult circumstances, the marriages of his children, and, above all, his gumption in talking in English to anyone of importance without knowing much English.

We asked him, 'Kaka, where did you learn English?'

'Me learning at my working, boyo.'

At the airport as a night watchman – his first job that brought him in direct contact with an Australian boss – it seems he was given the task of guarding a crane that dredged sand from the river for the building of the tarmac.

One night, it rained, cows and bulls, said Bro; the crane disappeared from the banks of the river. Bro hadn't kept a watch, so next morning he saw it down a few chains from its original position, the crane under the swirling waters of an angry river, only the top visible.

'Boyo, mountain flooding, waterfalling. Me guarding the bloody zhaam, crane. Morning I no see zhaam I going mad. What me telling the chutia Bosso when he coming? I run up and down. I see in Kalpu's kund, the top of zhaam showing. All things under water. I no guarding, night sleeping with your Kaki. I swim flooding river to zhaam. Climbing the top and sticky there like glue. On top, right on top, boyo. I hanging like a bat, upside down. The supervisor come in army jeep. The sahib he look me over. He taking his sun helmet off. His red mouth wide open like a monkey chutter, bum. He say, Ram, down man, coming down! I say, 'No, boss. It's me dootie. Sahib shout, You die there, Ram. All night you sitting there? I say humbly, Yes, bosso. The sahib crying. Me weeping too loudly.'

Indeed, the overseer was so impressed by Bro's dedication to duty that he pleaded, promising him a week's holiday on full pay.

Now Bro said, 'But, sahib, me no swimming.'

Then the supervisor sent some Fijian boys in a motor boat to winch

Bro off the submerged crane. And as Bro scrabbled on to the dry bank, his Fijian friend, Lesu, had hissed under his breath, 'Kaisi, kaiindia! Sa lasu! Lia lia. (Stupid Indian, telling lies!)'

'Barchod, chutia, Kaiviti,' hissed Bro with a grin.

Bro kept us regaled with his many exploits as we finished two bottles of local gin with fresh lemon from the trees growing behind my brother's corrugated-iron house, and spicy duck curry as chasers. Most of his stories dealt with his uncanny ability to outwit the European or the Chinese, or Chini as he called them. He saw no distinction between an Australian, a Kiwi or Englishman. All were White to his eyes. He told of his first visit to Suva, where at night he'd knocked on the wrong door only to be chased by a Chinese woman with a broom while her husband poured a pail of hot water from the top floor, scalding his screaming wife. Bro had escaped into the darkness.

'All houses looking the same to me in Suva,' he commented.

The highlight of his life was a cane growers' meeting at Regent Hotel, Fiji's five-star hotel built on the edge of Nadi. Bro had gone as a delegate from his cane harvesting gang: he had driven his tractor close to the hotel complex, and parked it behind a bush.

Bro marched to the foyer of the hotel and no one welcomed him or objected. Then he bought a couple of quick whiskies only to realise in another room the drinks were being served free by Fijian waiters paid for by the cane farmers. In an hour, he was high, so he ventured into another larger room where all kinds of delicious cakes and desserts were arranged. He began devouring.

Then he saw people going into the adjacent room led by a local chief. Bro hid his tray under a chair and followed the party. There, inside the large panelled room, was laid a feast fit for kings. Bro had begun his lunch with desserts; now he let himself go.

'Boys, I'm eating like a suwar pig. Like Taniela.'

When Chief Napoleoni Dawai saw him, he said kindly, 'Hey, Ram, BulaVinaka, Tamana. Have more, turanga. You pay for this, you know.'

Bro said Ratu Napoleoni was dead and the Regent now belongs to the Japanese. 'But, boyo, me never eating like that day. Phew! Farting all the way home!'

It was late now. Bro left us around midnight, walking through the night on an unforgettable path he had walked on so often like an old ox pulling the plough in the same furrow.

Next morning, my brother and his wife flew to Auckland, their first journey into another country, amidst another people amongst whom so many of our own had found a home.

*

The Nadi Tennis Club was exclusively for its white members, just as their swimming pools and other clubs had been a few decades ago. Then a few Indians and Fijians were allowed in, sponsored by the members, and depending on their annual income. So when I went to play tennis there on Saturday afternoon, two nights after my arrival, the place was full of Indian members, their wives and children splashing in the pool. The players were mainly young Indian businessmen and a few teachers. I recognised a few.

On my way to Suva, through the one-street Nadi Town, where Sukhdeo's wooden shop and Angie's café were, now stood a tall three-storey concrete building, the Bank of Baroda. On the second floor, my lawyer friend from Suva was running his lucrative law practice. During the first coup and between the two coups, Jasbir and his partner John Cameron had risked a lot to get us out of the colonel's clutches. Soon after, Jasbir had gone to Wellington with his wife and subsequently returned to resume his practice in Nadi.

John Cameron was somewhere in Perth and was not allowed recently to enter Fiji to attend a friend's funeral. No one among the lawyers or politicians seemed to care. 'We're only minting money,' said one proudly; the gadgets in Jasbir's office patently showed it. So we talked briefly of establishing a human rights and civil liberties group. We've never had anything like that in Fiji and the nightmare of the coups may yet be repeated. The guardians of law had simply become witnesses to the persecution. Then after a cup of coffee, and my admiration for the gadgets, I was on my way to Suva, the capital city of Fiji. Jasbir was contemplating his recent purchase – a sophisticated fax machine on top of which was the framed photograph of his baby girl born in Wellington.

As you drive out of the one-street town, just a little beyond the tramlines you are suddenly confronted by a massive new structure on the left. It rises like a Wordsworthian cliff. Subramanyam temple, Fiji's largest, is under construction. It is being designed on traditional architecture of the colourful South Indian temples. And many of the artisans carving images and idols have come from South India. Once built, it wouldn't only be a place of worship for the thousands of Hindus but a major tourist attraction.

The people of Fiji have always had a healthy religious sense until the fundamentalist Christians hijacked the Methodists with incitement from their coup cohorts. But there was a method in the Methodist madness. They set fire to a few temples, mosques and gurudwaras.

Among the rich Hindus, the religious fervour before the coups was one of prosperity. With all its myriad manifestations of spirituality, Hinduism is essentially of this material world: to people deprived, a life of things adds substantiality and permanence to an otherwise uncertain world. One had to thank god or gods for every blessing. During my father's generation, Saraswati, the goddess of learning and wisdom, was paramount; now it was Lakshmi, the goddess of wealth. Everything was economic, that's where the real power lay. We walked the streets of Suva feeling we had created it all until ten masked gunmen and a third-ranking colonel shattered the illusion. Once again, our fatalism found expression in our religion.

Gandhi had understood this phenomenon brilliantly. He got the richest support from the fabulously wealthy banias of India and, as a final penance, was assassinated by a high-caste extremist Hindu in the grounds of a 'temple' made for the Mahatma. The killer, not like unlike the Fijian colonel, thought he was a patriot.

Philosophically in Fiji, in the circumstances, it was understandable to me. There was little else to inspire hope or faith. But as I drove past that large structure, I wondered why we, as a people, had failed to create a newspaper or a university, so vital for any community that had so much image-building to do and possessed so little land.

Some Hindus are multimillionaires in Fiji but would they donate money to build a university or start an education foundation when a whole generation of Indian children are going without training? And now to be without higher education in Fiji is to become urchins of the second colonialism, only this time of the elite, privileged natives, some who wielded power without responsibility towards more than half the citizens of Fiji.

Hindu religiosity should be based not on the idea that God is on our side but whether we're on God's side. The ostentatiousness of a mawkish religiosity, evaporates like methylated spirit, heady for a while, not a trace afterwards. And it is always ominous. Gandhi knew that too but couldn't escape its hold on the Indian psyche. Perhaps that's why the partitions of Mother India's heart?

*

With these thoughts, I arrived at Cuvu secondary school, built two decades ago by the farmers of that area. Now it's a large secondary school catering for the needs of Indian and Fijian children. The principal is my first cousin Mr R.N. Deo. We'd grown up together. The head of English was another friend who had studied with me in Delhi. I was very keen to see them both and their wives. I had coffee with them and then Mr Kumar took me to his senior English classes, where two of my short stories were being taught. A real writer, no matter how small, creates a buzz in a school. So I was introduced and I talked about the stories: how to read and write them. Fiji, I said, was an unwritten world. But their life and the lives of their parents, grandparents, neighbours were worthy of being written about. Writing gave a special reality to their life. To write was to understand more than one life or a lifetime; to create a new reality and enter it through one's imagination.

The questions came with shyness and a literate sharpness. How lucky, I felt, the students were: Fijians and Indians, boys and girls, studying together, taught by a few qualified teachers. This was the most creative act of subversion against the regime that wanted separation on racial lines without knowing that there was an inseparable humanity of the human bondage. Besides, they were studying my stories. I'd grown up at that age on 'Daffodils' and 'The Lady of Shallot'. And studying the words containing their lives, they'd understand that the shroud of political apartheid won't last too long. Underneath the racist kafan, life would stir with the magic of imagination as roots in spring after winter.

It is in a similar school that I'd done my Senior Cambridge which had catapulted me on endless journeys of mind and migration. Secondary education was truly a historic Indian achievement against all kinds of odds and obstacles of colonial domination where race determined your destiny. Where ignorance was bliss.

A few kilometres from Cuvu Secondary School is Sigatoka town – a dilapidated little place known primarily as the birthplace of two Indian multimillionaires: Hari Punja and Kanti Tappoo. They began their shops in Sigatoka and prospered all over Fiji. Hari was my classmate up to Senior Cambridge. Kanti Tappoo married one of my students and I had taught two of his brothers – both professional people, one an engineer-writer and the other a lawyer-singer. I was quite fond of them. They, Suresh and Mahend, have remained my dear friends.

In a grey, shabby concrete building, Sir Vijay had his office on the second floor. I found him seated on a varnished wooden chair with a rough-hewn table in front. A fan was whirring at his feet and he was wiping sweat from his forehead. It was hot, humid – the weather after the cyclone when the sky is empty of all its tenderness and shines like a copper plate. A fly buzzed against an unopened, uncleaned window. We'd a brief chat: he was embittered by the reception from his friends when he returned. He mentioned a few prominent names with deep bitterness. New politics had taken its toll: it was rough, mean and moneyed. I had had so many dinners at his home made by his most hospitable wife Maya. I invited him for lunch; he declined, saying he was dieting. He did look slimmer than before. We left him scrutinising a brown file. He was a fine lawyer and had been the attorney-general in the Alliance government. Although I didn't know him well, he had been extremely brave during the coup. I wondered how long it would take before Sir Vijay bounced back; anyone who knew him knew that he had the ability of entering the revolving door of politics behind you and coming out in front.

The flood-damaged Sigatoka bridge was dammed to allow cars to pass on it. The river still whirled with thick muddy water. We managed to squeeze our Toyota across a precarious path. Once we were on the other side and as soon as the sugar cane fields disappeared in the lush bush, the scenery changed: it was greener hills and danker valleys; the devastating impact of Cyclone Kina was scarcely visible on the vegetation, though the houses looked battered, the palm trees swayed with broken fronds, and landslides had gashed the face of many a hill.

Cyclone Kina had hit Fiji a few weeks before with terrible fury: the floods and winds people had not known for sixty years: it was worse than the 'bara toofaan' – the big hurricane of which my grandparents had talked about in our childhood. After Rabuka's coups, Fiji didn't experience any significant natural disaster; the fundamentalist Fijians said the Lord was happy with the colonel's treachery. Now, after Kina, some Indians were saying, '*Bhagwan ke insaaf mein der hai, andher nahin*. In God's justice there may be delay but not injustice.'

Except that cyclone Kina had deconstructed everybody. And as you whizzed past on the sea road, you felt the deep vulnerability of island life. Islands were traps and we were marooned. Indian farms, Fijian villages where all were poor, what could be gained? Shadows of young men and women standing by the road, stretching their malnourished arms with a coconut or a crab dangling from them. We drove past like tourists in Japanese cars, winding up and down their windowpanes as the sellers waved and shouted to sell their meagre produce for a few paltry dollars.

As we approached Suva, it began drizzling: I've always liked a soft rain falling; it curtains the rest of the world from you. On this road, from Nadi to Suva, I'd travelled often: sometimes in a bus or in a friend's car; later as a lecturer at USP in my own first car, a Toyota with the number plate T701. I used to think life was like this winding road: the long patches dust-laden; then suddenly tar-sealed near the Fijian koros and small towns; the ups and downs of bare hills and green river valleys; Indian sugar cane farms; Fijian villages where hawkers sold coconuts, bananas, pawpaws, vegetables and bundles of fish, crabs, prawns and lobsters; then by the ever colour-changing ocean, green and blue, white and dark, in its freshness and moods like some large, subterranean life: salt water and land making love.

By the time we arrived home, the boot was filled with a week's food and smell. I'd picked up this habit from my father's days: he always carried a gunny sack, CSR company's stolen sugar bags. When he returned to Nadi town, the sack was full of seafood and vegetables. And in the town, we dreaded seeing him, for we were obliged to carry the sack home on our backs, after the Votualevu Junction bus stop.

Driving on the road shining black as a snake, I felt a sense of desolation in my heart. Rain often does that to me. A darkness was sitting on the vegetation like a wet vulture waiting. I became conscious of a kind of dying in paradise – a paradise stolen by thieves. By force of circumstance and force, our sense of reality had been brutalised, denied; our humanity as a people dispossessed, dismembered. It was a world that was dislocated, displaced; only the colonel and some Fijian chief were in place, secure. Or so they thought.

I'd known the largeness of heart, the openness of the Fijian landscape and its many possibilities. Perhaps islands were traps but not our island: it was unique. If one had failed or faltered, there was still a shared destiny. Now, I felt, we'd separate, shattered destinations. Fiji was going through a season of anomie: from a myth of paradise it had degenerated into a metaphor of lying. The texture and culture of a world we'd lost. Others had betrayed; we, or I, had banished myself. So many had gone away with so much disgust. Incredibly this has happened in Fiji. We should have never accepted it.

But there was peace: you could drive from Nadi to Suva without soldiers molesting you or thugs bashing your car with stones. That decency in Fiji on which we'd grown, which we cherished, was still there, even if frayed at the edges or torn inside oneself. Was it fear or was it something in the Fijian-Indians – some fragment of their ancient, essentially tolerant and peaceful tradition that they had become aware of under provocation and intimidation and suffering.

Gandhi had lighted it and illuminated the world with it: significantly, he'd begun among the indentured Indians in South Africa. Ironically, South Africa was recovering its lost self while in the South Pacific we were beginning a wretched journey, of all places, in Fiji.

But Fiji, so far, had avoided an ethnic conflict of the kind one reads about in the death pockets of Asia, Africa, Arabia, America and Europe. This was a large achievement in a small country. Maybe people had begun to understand each other's fears. Or maybe it was a belief that one's weakness can be one's greatest strength. That there are ways of solving conflicts, even with colonels, that can be creative and more enduring. And all that took time, sometimes a very long time. Politics, after all, was an interminable undertaking; its invisible companion is hope: a four-letter word, just another word for life. Even love, one hoped. Or just FIJI.

*

We turned left at the corner of Suva Cemetery: the place where the sign says 'Welcome to Suva City' and behind it 'The Wages of Sin is Death'. The Reservoir Road took me to Prince's Road where, at the corner, the Commonwealth of Australia was building a huge high commission complex. A little beyond on the right stood India House, the residence of the Indian high commissioner, so vengefully closed by the military regime. I had had many happy evenings in that house, where the generosity of the Indians knew no bounds. No politician in Fiji now talked about the abomination of closing the high commission that had given so much to the people of Fiji: even Rabuka had studied in India; so had I when opportunities for Fiji children were few and far between.

A little up the Prince's Road, Jyoti and I had built our house in 1984. I'd jokingly called it 'A House for Mr Biswas' for I'd bought the land from a friend at a cocktail party; another had found me a contractor, soon after I was sacked from the university after my election to parliament in 1982. And a house for Mr Biswas it became. We had lived in it for barely thirteen months. However, it had given me a lot of joy when that Christmas, Jyoti's mother Ivy came to stay with us from Delhi. She had also planted in the front garden the pine tree we had used as a Christmas tree. The tree had grown tall and slender and very green in Suva's abundant rain.

When Ivy was there, she had also experienced her first hurricane. I remember how she had walked from room to room as the wind howled, roared and crashed; the sea was dark and wild and the cyclonic clouds scuttled the sky like chariots of war. Our house shook but not a glass pane broke. The two gnarled pine trees didn't fall. And around midnight, as Ivy prayed, it was all calm. I thought this was Ivy, at seventy-five, experiencing her eye of the storm not unlike Elizabeth Hunter in Patrick White's famous novel *The Eye of the Storm*.

Looking at this house from outside, I felt quite detached. It had been rented for the past few years. The pine tree which Ivy had planted had been cut and removed. The bougainvilleas in the garden were mutilated. There was no overwhelming emotion in me, although it was the only piece of property and land my wife and I had owned in Fiji. The roof of the house needed a new coat of paint. I didn't go inside; many of my books were still there; instead, I decided to sell it to my tenants. Perhaps a moment's stupendous decision. Within three days, it was sold and I was, once again, homeless in paradise.

*

As you drive down Prince's Road, then Edinburgh Drive towards Suva city, there's a notice which says 'Disasters do Happen. Are you Prepared?' Then you begin to see such notices all over the grimy city. I've never been quite at home in Suva: it is Nadi that has been my hometown. But I lived in Suva for almost twenty years. I met a few former political colleagues; the unelected deputy speaker invited me for lunch at the new Parliament House which was then in session.

I declined, saying that I wouldn't go there until a non-Fijian, too, could dream of holding the highest elected office in the land. At the moment, they were constitutionally barred. The old parliament chamber had been forgotten in the grey pile of imperial stones. In that old, colonial building, I had been aware of the tensions as well as the vitality of our society – small, complex and dynamic. In it, I'd a sense of place and grace. There had been no menace of militarism until the day of the coup. I had no desire to see the new Parliament House built on the foundation of guns literally called the Battery Hill.

The parliament in session was a babel of racial politics. It must have been hell to listen daily to racist vilifications in what should have been the voice of conscience in the land. From 'Amen' to 'Idi Amin' is a short distance, I'd said rather impetuously in the old parliament. The obscenities of political racialism makes a certain kind of individual extremely eloquent: from Enoch Powell, a professor of Greek, to the semi-literate saviours of Caliban's tribe. Power tends to corrupt but the fear of the absence of power, I think, corrupts absolutely.

What should have been a house of prayer was descending into a den of thieves.

Meeting so many people – lawyers, academics, politicians, farmers, businessmen – one got the sinking feeling that a relentless culture of corruption was in the making, an invisible chain of injustice had been forged. No serious talk of reconciliation, reconstitution or regeneration. To get a birth certificate, you had to pay $10 to a clerk; for a business licence a little more. Was it really that bad? 'Yes,' came the chorus of answers. 'Right at the top, the rot has set in.' Such a perception of political and business life by professional people was disturbing. It led to cynicism and finally to self-contempt. It's the unenviable, inevitable consequence of a coup in any part of the Third World.

'Look around, pal,' they whispered. 'Who's building? Who's expanding the shops? Check the directors' list. The hospitals remain neglected like mortuaries.'

The nouveaux riche, together with the coup men and a few politicians, were doing well through intrigue and financial corruption. People who had been through two unnecessary coups and the consequent uncertainties and insecurities, both at personal and communal levels, didn't want to be caught again without money. Power itself was not much but to be in a position to buy power with cash and manipulate those who thought they had power was to be more powerful. It was the power of the powerless. Every man (and not a few women) had his price. The liquor of power smelt strong in those flared nostrils while some looked like His Master's Voice dog, peering in stupefaction down the horn of the gramophone from which a nasty sound came.

During my visit, Fiji's a most atrocious business fraud was making headlines. A notorious businessman was in the process of defrauding the national coffers of around $10 million. In just the nick of time, his hand was caught in the till, his accomplices identified. The parliament ordered an inquiry. Nothing had been done for months. Now the fraud was saying, with approval from his powerful accomplices, that there should be no inquiry as this would waste taxpayers' money, especially when every dollar was required for rehabilitating the people after cyclone Kina! There was no limit to the crook's hypocrisy. People laughed: there was no indignation or contempt nor even muffled outrage in the media.

*

Next day, I went to visit a few colleagues at the university where I had spent almost twenty years. The university still remained, in the South Pacific, a place of hope and exploration and an oasis for both students and staff. New buildings stood casting long, dull shadows. The foliage was verdure and thick. Tupeni Baba, my colleague and the education minister in the Bavadra cabinet, was now installed in my room: I was delighted to hear his laughter. He said I may have saved his life on the day of the coup. His interest in politics had waned since the death of Dr Bavadra and the dissolution of the coalition. But he had now become the co-owner of some exclusive apartments called Elixir, where most politicians stayed during the parliamentary sessions.

'You must see it, Satend,' he said with solid pride.

A floor below Tupeni's office was Sudesh Mishra, one of Fiji's new poets. Sudesh had just published his second book, *Tandava*, named after Shiva's dance of death. At least Shiva was still dancing – most things seemed so dead to me.

I asked for Raymond Pillai and Subramani, two short story writers: Pillai had gone to Wellington; Subramani was in Sydney writing a novel. Then I saw Pio Manoa, a Chinese-Fijian poet of deep talent. The Fiji playwright Jo Nacola, the most creative Fijian academic and whose contract was not renewed by his department and who became the minster for natural resources in Dr Bavadra's cabinet, had made a political comeback. He was the minister for ethnic and multicultural affairs. Vilisoni Heneriko, another playwright of some promise, had been compelled by a couple of mediocre academics to take a flight to Hawaii.

I went to the university bookshop and bought almost all the publications by local writers and left. I was surprised that there was no feeling of nostalgia in me as I walked about the campus I had known like my village. Those who had denied me a job had unwittingly given me freedom, which I prized now above all else. And my young friend, P.R. Sharma, the longest-serving member of the university's general staff, had committed suicide after his lean-to home was burnt by his neighbour. The tanoa in his room remained empty and dry. My golden codgers – Som, Subhas and Nand, the illustrious cardplayers – had all gone.

*

I drove around a bit to have a good look at the campus houses I'd lived in – four in all. My favourite home was our first house given to me when I joined USP as one of its first local lecturers in February 1969. The house was still there, shutters up, paint peeling and the lawns around it unmowed. The yellow-flowered vine I'd planted on the side wall was mutilated by the recent cyclone. Above the house was a little, bare hillock, next to a deep ravine. From this high spot, one could see the blue Pacific rolling evermore in its peaceful majesty – no postcard or tourist brochure could do justice to the beauty and the infinitely changing moods and colours of a magnificent ocean. One had to understand its eternal rhythm, the monotonous beatings of its mighty heart like the wind in waves.

Early mornings, I used to go for walks down Catalina Road and then on to the Queen Elizabeth Drive, by the seashore, that semicircled the city of Suva and enclosed the university. Perhaps for the first time I was becoming aware of the breathtaking loveliness of an island. Our villages were made of little farms on which we worked for a meagre sustenance. There was little time to see Nature in its manifold variety: our lives were so full of daily care that we truly had no time to stand and stare. But from this campus I was beginning to see the sea which until then hadn't meant much to me: its exquisite rippling waves.

Walking by the sea early in the morning was a revelation: the gentle breeze, the waves lapping the craggy edges, the sun bursting over the ocean, a few small boats returning after a night's fishing, a couple of Fijian women sitting on the large, black, barnacled boulders casting their lines for something for breakfast while their children splashed in the receding tide. But it was only now, standing on that bare hill, that the lines came back to me with a new and searing understanding:

> O well for the fisherman's boy
> That he shouts with his sister at play
> O well for the sailor lad
> That he sings in his boat in the bay!

I'd read and memorised this lyric as a secondary schoolboy. More than thirty years later, I was beginning to sense its sorrows when more than the sea had broken. The epiphany of the morning had given way to a darkness in the sun: and so much was illuminated like sunlight on broken columns.

*

It was on this campus that I'd met so many white men and women. My children had played with their children and the children of the Fijian housegirls who lived in their one room bures, adjacent to the houses. Rohan was four, Gita three; Jyoti had begun teaching at a secondary school named after Gandhi.

I was beginning to take my own teaching seriously and befriended a generous Kiwi by the name of Lincoln Gribble. He'd a Maltese wife and they had three beautiful daughters and a son. Our house was surrounded by other houses with married couples and children. And as so often happens, you discover some of the best people through your young kids. We were invited to every party, possibly then as the only coloured academic couple at the university. If this was tokenism, I missed its subterranean significance. I was too happy and young to worry about subtexts of a life beginning for me and my young family in a new world opening.

Next to our house arrived a young English psychologist with a younger wife. Mickey was clever and articulate with a Cheshire cat grin; his wife was the envy of most of the Kiwi wives, not so much because of her youthful abandon, but her habit of sunning herself on the green lawns in the barest of bikinis on a white towel tempting the sun. Kiwis walked past her as she lay blissfully indifferent to the consternation she'd caused among the other white women who had never been to London. A few years later when I returned from my further studies, I was saddened to hear that she and Mickey had separated: she was living in Toorak with an islander while Mickey had gone to Hong Kong to teach psychology to the Chinese in the last, lost colony of Little England.

One of my great joys was the frequent visits of my parents to USP from my village. Whenever he felt like it, my father would take the Pacific Transport bus and arrive at the Suva market. There he'd buy bundles of crab, fish, prawns and bhaji. He'd then hire a taxi and arrive at our door in great style. Sometimes he'd be accompanied by mother but when Amma was not there, he invited a nagonchi by the name of Niranjan.

Who this mysterious companion of my father was, I never discovered. It was enough that he was my father's friend – perhaps a grog-drinking mate. Only now I realise that maybe he was the only person my father knew in Suva and with whom he stayed whenever he came to this city to bring my mother to the CWM hospital for an illness that needed a specialist's diagnosis.

Now that I was in Suva, perhaps my father wanted to repay that kindness in some measure or even to show off a bit as his son was now living in a bungalow among so many white men, and Niranjan remained a stranger to us except when on some Saturdays I saw him in the Suva market and gave him money to buy his lunch. But he never came to our house on the campus on his own. The place had always been out of bounds for such men and women, not unlike my parents. It was a Royal NZ Air Force base before; now a university, equally forbidding and forbidden to those we so thoughtlessly call ordinary men, and Niranjan and Father sat on the mat drinking grog and keeping an eye on Mickey's wife, while Jyoti and Parvati were busy preparing a feast in the kitchen. Rohan and Gitanjali played on the steps while I sat on one of the two canvas chairs provided by the university. It used to give me great joy to see my father enjoying himself in such salubrious surroundings and occasionally casting a furtive glance at Mickey's wife lying in the evening sun. Every time a car passed by or someone ran past our house towards the swimming pool, they would wave at me. Father would respond with an expansive gesture of his own. Even Niranjan attempted his own salutations to the women who passed by in their scanty swimsuits.

There were days when my two children held their grandfather's hands and went for a stroll on the campus road. Father in his blue-striped underwear made by Ratanji Tailors (London-trained) walking tall in between his tiny grandchildren.

Then I went away to England to study and a while later to Canberra. While I was in Canberra, Father suffered a massive stroke that paralysed him. My young doctor brother kept him alive for almost four years and then one night after midnight I got a call from my sister-in-law that Father had died in his sleep.

I sat in the room that Father had sat and slept in in the campus house. All I could think of was how to announce his death on the radio the next day. For me, my father had died almost four years ago: now we had to cremate the skeletal remains of a very big man. Life can be so long; forgetting even longer. And yet he'd been more of Fiji than anyone else in my family: my grandparents were born in India; we'd travelled to other worlds. His generation alone, born and bred in Fiji, were now buried and cremated there too. They had not known any other land; their children had become no land's men and women.

*

Slowly I drove around the campus looking at several other houses where I'd known a few friends – all of whom had left now for other destinations. I myself had lived in four houses at one time or another and now scarcely recognised the new occupants.

I knew these houses would haunt me as I watched the flight of a bird across the sea searching for another island nest. It is on this campus I'd first met and taught so many young men and women from the South

Pacific islands. They had opened my world to other worlds. Among them, I'd known great affection and fun which the young give so unstintingly as we push them into the tunnels of our learned prejudices.

That afternoon, I visited the place where I had been hidden for four days during the second coup on 25 September. Even my wife didn't quite know where I had disappeared. That had become the joke of my friends who had been caught napping and taken to Naboro prison, Fiji's notorious prison for most hardy criminals.

My young brother had built his house a street away. He was no longer there: he'd sold it cheaply and gone to Auckland because his contract as the university's deputy librarian had been in jeopardy. Supporters of the coup and sycophants then ruled the roost: self-respect demanded departure for many.

In the evening, I was back in Nadi, and with my mother and brother, visited my second village, Legalega, where I had spent my youth. The village was there but my two brothers, a sister and so many of my childhood friends had migrated: we sat and counted, almost a hundred. My mother remembered every name, which pleased me as it showed she was quite aware and well and her memory was sharp as a cane-knife. Now she lived in Nadi town, but the faces of the village grieved in her. Her orchard had disappeared: the jungle cut, made into a field, which lay fallow. For a moment, I felt, if the Indians left Fiji, it would be as terrible as a landscape without trees.

*

Early next morning, I'd to the catch the early bird flight. As my young brother got ready, my mother made a cup of tea. Saying goodbye to an almost eighty-year old mother was not easy and mothers never say goodbye to their children gladly, just as no child ever leaves his mother.

My brother drives me to the airport. As we pass the houses, still asleep, I see the damage the cyclone had wrought; but on trees, leaves were sprouting again. If only coups, too, were like cyclones, there'd be some hope of regeneration. But the casual brutality of a coup and the cunning betrayals of men take longer to heal than nature's karmic dharma.

I drive past the village faintly visible in pre-dawn darkness, so deceptively and disturbingly quiet and so full of so many damaged lives. But darkness doesn't always destroy the thing it conceals.

The airport is well lit, our flight is on time; the duty-free shop is well stocked. The place was painted in chappanchoori colours: the woman who symbolised Nadi town during my secondary school days.

Our aircraft soars into the bursting dawn over blue hills and green cane fields. The tawdry little village-town is awash in half-light. Suddenly I think of 'Josephine' – is she, too, returning home? Then our plane was above the clouds like an island lost in the undivided, indifferent ocean-sky, with a sadness that covered us all.

*

I take out Brian Keenan's *An Evil Cradling* from my satchel and read.

> I remembered one of the prison cells I had been kept in. I awoke early in the morning hearing the dawn call to prayer and suddenly jumped up screaming and swearing as I swept the ants from my flesh. Hundreds and hundreds seasonally invaded the cells in which we were kept. Like the giant Gulliver in a rage of frustration and cold sweat I would stamp and slap and crush them without mercy without any thought of their separate existence. But after days of this I got tired of my anger. It exhausted me.
>
> The ants were inexhaustible. I began searching out where they entered the cell, blocking up small cracks and fissures with bits of wet tissue or broken matchsticks, but they would always find another point of entry. As I watched them pour into the cell through so many different places they became for me a form of entertainment. I watched them work. I watched how they would search out a crumb of bread four or five times their own size. They would trail and pull or push this piece of bread the full length of my tiny cell, scale a vertical wall, crawl along ridges until they had found an exit point and take with them what they had found.

My fascination made friends of them. I was grateful for their fortitude, their strength, for their resilience and instead of raging at them I would sit awaiting their return. I watched how they worked together. And how, if I had crushed one in the night by accident, the others would gather around and if there was life in it still, a comrade would lift this wounded companion and carry it across for what to these tiny creatures must have seemed like miles, crawl up the vertical wall and search out an escape point through which they could take this maimed insect to be amongst its own. This incident became a symbol for me in this blank room with its three chained creatures. We cannot abandon the injured or the maimed, thinking to ensure our own safety and sanity. We must reclaim them, as they are part of ourselves.

*

Sydney was buzzing with life. The flight to Canberra was brief: I sat next to a heavy man with a big file. It was the beginning of a new season in my adopted city. My favourite writer Patrick White had called it 'the most unreal city in Australia, unripe with the hypocrisy of politics and diplomacy'. I was glad he'd left out the groves of academe. As my son Rohan drove me in his car from the airport, I saw the first leaves turning to gold. But just for a moment, seeing my son, I felt the first sensations of home and homelessness.

It was, after all, autumn – an experience I'd not known in Fiji, an epiphany of age and youth, father and son, loss and longing, driving on a new road, its edges strewn and stippled with dry, yellow leaves fallen like grievances: only the transplanted trees would soon stand starkly bare like grief itself. But to flower in spring it had to survive a leafless winter, a season unknown in Fiji. Winter had to be borne; grief lived; a new landscape loved; and a house built; a home created.

And the falling of a leaf described in words and life seen in a single tear.

5. A Remembrance

Ian Donaldson (16 May 1935–18 March 2020)

In these grief-stricken times, there's a great grief in my heart.

Grazia wrote today, an hour ago, that Ian, her partner, had died. The news of death didn't shock me, for at my age so many familiar faces disappear into the night as if the lights, one by one, are being switched off before you go to sleep. Their voices become silent forever, except hauntingly surfacing in your memory or a dream.

But death is an ineluctable reality: no matter how expected, it leaves a void deep inside your being. Mortality connects us too intimately. Someone precious has gone and you'll never again feel the touch of that vanished hand or receive an email, a card on your birthday, or a phone call from him or her. Or share a cup of morning tea, or a mug of coffee in the afternoon.

Life is finite; the loss of a loved life leaves a sense of the infinite emptiness. Zeros don't have value once the One is erased.

*

A few months ago, Ian, Grazia, Jyoti and I had lunch in a Canberra hotel. I'd met Ian accidentally in the Petherick Reading Room of the National Library, where he was working on a book. I invited him for lunch with Grazia and Jyoti. Grazia was researching her biographical narrative of the National Gallery.

Ian seemed to enjoy the meal but there was a strange quietness about him. His smile had lost its alluring charm. After a leisurely lunch, as we walked downstairs, Grazia whispered to Jyoti that Ian wasn't quite well. In fact, he was 'seriously ill'. He had been through two heart bypasses: 'It may take a while before he recovers fully,' she told my wife.

Meeting him that day and seeing him talking, walking, I wouldn't have guessed it, for he was his usual solicitous soul. Since he knew the family, he enquired what our three children, Rohan, Gitanjali and Kavita, were doing. We exchanged family notes as we, too, knew his and Tamsin's two children, Ben and Sadie.

As we said goodbye, we promised to meet more often when they came back to Canberra in 2020.

*

It was on the ANU campus that I had first met Professor Ian Donaldson in 1975. I'd arrived from Fiji, with Jyoti and our three children, to study for my doctorate in English. It was the beginning of wintry weather in Canberra; coming from a tropical island, we weren't quite prepared for it embraced us with its cold and flu. The family fell ill for a fortnight in the brick house on Miller Street, not far from the ANU campus.

Later, I was given a scholar's room in Childers Street. There were other postgraduate students: we congregated for coffee every morning. One wet afternoon one of them announced that the A.D. Hope building would be ready soon and some of us might get rooms in it. I'd read Hope's poetry years ago, but didn't know a monument in concrete was being built to be named after this most cerebral of Australian poets.

Being the only, possibly the first, non-European doctoral scholar in the then English Department, I was given a lovely little room in the A.D. Hope building. The room had a large window and two large cottonwood trees grew next to it. For the first time, I felt warm. The sun came streaming in the mornings. There were three other rooms near my room with younger scholars, one from as far as Canada, named Diana.

It was in this room that I wrote my three short stories, 'A Pair of Black Shoes', 'The Guru' and 'The Tree': the first two widely read in Fiji secondary schools for the past forty years.

At one end of the building, on the first floor, were all the professors and lecturers of English: W.S. Milgate, A.D. Hope, John Hardy, Bill Ramson, Judith Wright, Bob Brissenden, Livio Dobrez, Fred Langman, David Parker and Graeme Clarke.

At the other end, overlooking the Black Mountain Tower with its Telstra syringe, was the new, spacious Humanities Research Centre. The windows were large and one could see the transplanted trees in scarlet and gold until the leaves were gone with winter's wild, whispering winds, leaving the ghostly gums standing in their ancient loneliness.

Years later, I was to remember the scene and titled my fourth book of poems, *The Loneliness of Islands*. It was in the room in the A.D. Hope building that I wrote my first slim volume of poems, *Faces in a Village*, recalling my days and nights refracted in the vanishing faces of villagers in Fiji. A generation was going, one by one. And I carried the slivers of a broken mirror to reflect their lives in my words.

*

The Humanities Research Centre was established in 1974. It was presumably the first of its kind in Australasia; Professor Ian Donaldson was appointed its foundation director. I didn't know anything about him but did see him walking in the corridors to go up to his large room filled with books with a few family photos. The door was always open as if inviting any visitor who might care to walk in for a chat or a cup of tea.

As postgraduate students, we organised a series of weekly seminars in Commonwealth Literature. I'd done my second Masters in this new realm of Literatures in English at Leeds. For me, it opened a fascinating world: literature written in the English Commonwealth; among them V.S. Naipaul whose *A House for Mr Biswas* I'd read in Fiji as a young teacher, almost a decade before I went to England to study.

In London during the summer, I read Patrick White's fiction, subsequently taught by William Walsh, the first Professor of Commonwealth Literature in the world. *The Tree of Man* and *Voss* opened the new world down under for me. I was so moved by these two Australian novels that I wished to do my PhD on Patrick White's fiction.

As luck would have it, in 1974, I was given a scholarship to study at the ANU. Gough Whitlam was the prime minister: bliss it was in that dawn to come to Australia! And Bob Brissenden, who had studied in Leeds, invited me to join him; Bob became my delightful and creative supervisor.

*

Patrick White's fiction and coming to Australia changed more than my destiny. It changed the trajectory of my wife's and my children's life too. The ANU became our place of study and joyful friendships. Kavita and Jyoti completed their doctorates almost in the same room that I'd occupied decades ago. Gitanjali and Rohan studied in other departments on the campus. Our granddaughter Hannah Maya is now a second year student in the Science Faculty.

*

Before coming to Australia, my knowledge of this island continent was minimal: images of fumigation at Sydney airport; a few Fijians sent back to Fiji for overstaying their visas; half-dressed Aussie tourists as the cruise liners touched Suva harbour among fully attired native Christians and immigrant Indians. *Fiji Times*, then our only daily, owned by an Australian, relished exposing all this in bold headlines with a sense of fun in the sun.

Australia was our biggest neighbour, but not close to our hearts and minds. Geography and history's migration bound us to the south Pacific Ocean but our culture and the habitus of living had little in common. England was closer to the Australians; India to many Fiji Indians; and rugby to the indigenous Fijians. White Australia added its own distances and dislocations.

I could point to Australia on a map but I'd neither emotional nor intellectual ties with the largest, most ancient island continent with its most extraordinary civilisation. Nor did I know much of Fiji's history or how my grandparents from near Lucknow (what Luck?) were cozened, recruited as indentured labourers to work on sugar estates owned by the CSR company of Sydney, Australia. They had never seen a ship or a sea wave but had been loaded and transported thousands of miles in sailing ships, with no sense of direction or destination. Their destiny was decided by others.

When they arrived in the South Seas, they were black British subjects and their children couldn't migrate to this vast, empty colony. From the obscure villages of a subcontinent they came and became Indian-Islanders of the most unusual kind. They worked and died in Fiji; they were cremated on the shores of the Pacific Ocean but always remained separate and unequal.

Whoever wrote 'All men are created equal' knew only half the truth; 'all are cremated equally' is perhaps closer to the whole truth!

*

I met Ian through our evening seminars – he attended mine on *A House for Mr Biswas* and sat through the discussion with an amused look. Who would, in the English Department of the Australian National University, have ever thought of giving a talk on a novel set in Trinidad, written by an indentured labourer's precocious grandson?

The book was over 500 pages long and written when Vidia Naipaul was barely twenty-nine years old. Apparently, no one had read the novel in the English Department when I gave my talk. But the discussion lasted until midnight: there was always an abundance of wine and cheese.

Next morning, Ian knocked on my door and invited me for lunch. Alec Hope and Bob Brissenden joined us – Hope with a rather large flagon of red wine: my baptism in Australian wines began that day.

A highlight in our celebration of Commonwealth literature was the visit of George Lamming, the Caribbean writer and critic of Vidia Naipaul's satirical novels. Jyoti and I arranged a dinner at our home in Hughes. Around twenty people came to meet and hear Lamming: we began at seven p.m. and the evening ended at around two a.m. Ian was there throughout listening to the Caribbean's conversation, almost as fascinating as Sobers's batting, but none of us was sober that night!

I began attending the many functions at the HRC and met remarkable scholars in the Humanities, who came as visiting fellows to the HRC for short periods. They enriched our lives in so many ways. The wines and cheeses were the best available in Canberra, with varieties of grapes. There was an embracing generosity and a warmth in the invitations.

To this day, I'm attached to the HRC, now in the Sir Ronald Wilson building. Sadly, the new building doesn't have the open largeness of the A.D. Hope, nor its design or architectural simplicity. But we can see through the coffee room windows across Lake Burley Griffin, the Parliament House shining in Canberra's slanting light: how often I remember the Fiji parliament and that darkness at noon imposed by a native colonel and ten masked gunmen! The picture of the National Library on the left, on the edge of the lake, is a reassuring ode of Grecian solidity.

In the new HRC, we do have a most welcoming poet-director in Professor Will Christie from Sydney. I'm attached to it. Jyoti is in an honorary position in the English Department. We go to the HRC almost every Tuesday for coffee with other visiting fellows and guests. We attend its varied activities followed by wine, cheese and fruits with an occasional dinner hosted by the director. We talk about our friends who have had connections with the centre.

A few years ago we celebrated Ian's eightieth birthday with many friends of yesteryear attending the function in the HRC precincts in the A.D. Hope building. It was for me a wonderful occasion to meet so many old friends who had retired. We had the dinner in Ian's honour on top of Red Hill. There I met Peter Rose, the enterprising and imaginative editor of the *ABR*.

*

It was Ian who wrote to me in October1987, after the two Fijian coups, inviting me to be a visiting fellow for a while at the HRC. More than most, he understood the difficulties I was having in Fiji, having lost two jobs in two days, incarcerated twice, and no prospect of another in Fiji – the perils of politics, the treason of soldiers and clerks. He had offered me a fellowship in the early 1980s to convert my thesis into a book but my petty ambitions in my little colony prevented me from accepting it. One can be trapped in islands like Naipaul's mimic men. But literature can open the world as nothing else can. It gives both courage and strength. One must go on, step by step, day by day, word by word, book by book: reading and writing, teaching and travelling.

The ANU was a wonderful experience for me: we had sent our son Rohan to study there. When Ian revived the fellowship, I had more than scholarly reasons to revisit Canberra.

I came with Jyoti, our two daughters, two suitcases, for a few months but stayed on for five long, long years without returning to Fiji. One world had disintegrated; another was taking shape; our lives changed. Bit by bit, we created a home.

It was Ian's letter that I'd taken, all alone, to the Fiji military barracks one afternoon, much to the surprise of the military officers and against the advice of my friends. It was there we were confined for the first day of the coup on 14 May 1987, from noon to midnight. There was the fear that I might be imprisoned again by an unsettled, nervous army that had perpetrated its treason at ten in the Fiji parliament in session. The Fiji Hansard records my interjection – 'Address the Chair–' as the last legitimate words before a 'stranger' walks in.

I must say I was treated with great courtesy by the officer-in charge at the Queen Elizabeth Barracks; he and his colleagues, after scrutinising

Ian's letter with his elegant signature, gave me permission to travel outside Fiji.

I left Nadi for Canberra within two days, lest the soldiers changed their mind and once again we were prevented from flying out from Nadi airport where I grew up grazing my Nani's cow named Lali and a horse named Charlie.

*

We came to Canberra in December 1987. Christmas came: we'd a most happy season – the kindness of so many people of the English Department and the HRC. After Christmas, Ian went on leave but left his car with us. By March 1988, as the CCAE was becoming a university, I got a job at the young university. Later, I was offered a more senior position by Professor John Hardy in Queensland, but I wanted to be in Canberra, a decision I've never regretted.

John was the head of English at the ANU when I completed my doctorate on 'The Image of the Artist in Patrick White's Fiction'. The thesis was submitted in December 1977. In April 1978, I was thrilled to receive his letter informing me of its acceptance without changing a word.

Ian invited me on a HRC fellowship to convert it into a book but by then I'd smaller political ambitions in my small country. Literature had given me some sense of non-racial politics and an idealism that literature can make a difference politically, and empower one to try to change the direction of political thinking with the words of other thinkers. That we succeeded so well led to the two military coups of 1987. In 1986, I'd become Fiji's first Labour MP. From 1978 I was writing speeches for opposition politicians and articles for newspapers. I was elected to Fiji parliament in April 1982 on NFP ticket.

*

Fiji was a small colony, ceded to Great Britain during the imperial century when the sun didn't set on the Empire. On 10 October 1874, Fiji became a Crown Colony. There, on the International Date Line, the sun rose first on the Empire.

Australian interests and British pragmatism soon led to the recruitment and transport of Indian indentured labourers for economic viability of the native colony, without disrupting the Fijian way life, ruled by the chiefs of Fiji, assisted, as usual, by the colonising advisors with their colonial inheritance. After all, they ruled India, a handful of them, by Indian help in abundance. The story was the same: only the colonies were different. Indenture, a step away from slavery, though, had a return date after a decade.

In 1879, the first Indians arrived in the Fijian archipelago: in 1893 M.K. Gandhi went to South Africa as a boy lawyer and was thrown out of his first-class compartment at Pietermaritzburg station, near Durban. Things were never the same again. In sixty years, the Empire changed and with it the world after the two world wars and the Russian Revolution. Young Gandhi had wrought his own miracles, however flawed.

*

So here I was in Canberra in 1988. Dr Timoci Bavadra, the deposed Labour PM, died in 1989. A memorial service was held in his honour at the ANU: Foreign Minister Gareth Evans and I spoke on the occasion. Ian must have heard my eulogy to a humble Fijian leader, a Vuniwai, a healer, a commoner of uncommon appeal. He invited me to the HRC and gave me a room to sit and write my story. I read, and wrote and taught at the University of Canberra. Every weekend I was in my office at the HRC. It was a most salubrious place with new horizons for me visible through those large glass windows with the winds in the trees outside. My friends at UC were generous and indulgent. I travelled often towards India and Europe.

During this period, I wrote *The Wounded Sea* (1991), which I dedicated to my Amma and Jyoti's mother, Ivy. *The Wounded Sea* had several wonderful reviews, perhaps because it was the first book of its kind to give some idea of a slice of Indian life in the South Pacific: most people didn't quite know that a community of Indians had lived in the South Seas for more than a century. It was a unique fragment of history, not experienced, I believe, on any other island.

The Wounded Sea was launched at the Canberra Word Festival 1991 by Don Dunstan and at Perth Writers Festival by my Fijian friend Vijay Mishra. Don had spent his formative years in Fiji among the descendants of indentured Indians and native chiefs. I'm at the moment reading his remarkable biography by Professor Angela Woollacott.

Ian wrote a letter to me after reading it.

How much I enjoyed *The Wounded Sea*. It's a marvellously eloquent and moving book…you write with wonderful feeling and humour, even of the grimmest events.

His words meant a lot to me.

Then I wrote my autobiography *Requiem for a Rainbow* (2001), and dedicated it to my late brother Mahendra and to Ian Donaldson. Ian was then a Professor of English in Cambridge, after his sojourn as the Regius Professor at the University of Edinburgh – I visited Edinburgh mainly to see where Jyoti's father had done his MA in English Literature, half a century ago, as a scholar from India.

Requiem was launched at the 2001 ACLALS meeting in Canberra by Bob McMullan, the then Labor shadow minister for Aboriginal affairs.

I completed these two volumes while being connected with the HRC. Both books brought rich rewards for a small writer. I spent more than two years in that HRC room in the A.D. Hope building while living in Cottage 16 on campus in the now Judith Wright's Corner, next to University House; in the vicinity is hidden among tress a larger-than-life statue of Winston Churchill.

If Ian had not invited me to the HRC and given me a room to write, I doubt I would have written anything or come to Canberra. And stayed on. The only other city I've loved is Delhi, where my wife grew up, where two of my children were born. And where Jyoti's beloved mother is buried. Nadi, the place of my birth, is still a tiny town often submerged in a tropical cyclone. Writing, bits and pieces, became a deeply healing process to my hurt heart.

While I was associated with the HRC, we founded the ACT PEN International with Ian's help and at the initiative of my friend, poet-scholar Dennis Haskell from Perth. We wanted Ian to be the foundation president of ACT PEN. He insisted I should take that position, having had some experience of prison in the two Fijian coups. PEN International ACT became an active group of several Canberra writers, each one dedicated to helping writers in prison in the region. Thomas Keneally sponsored an annual lecture at the NLA: it lasted for a dozen or so years and we established stone memorials for imprisoned writers in Lennox Park by the lake. Once I left for Fiji, a couple of years later, ACT PEN became part of the Sydney PEN.

*

After seventeen years in Canberra, Jyoti and I were invited to Fiji to help establish Fiji's second university for the poor. We resigned from our universities and returned to Lautoka, a harbour city next to the Nadi airport.

We invited Ian Donaldson to become our external advisor in English Studies in the School of Humanities and the Arts of which I was the foundation dean. Ian accepted our fledgling university's offer. He came and spent a week with us: talked to our village students and the staff. and gave a public lecture, and saw Fiji's volcanic landscapes as we took him around – it was his first visit to the islands.

He wrote a thoughtful report for the future of English teaching at our university. I doubt if Fiji ever had a more distinguished professor of English visiting its shores and showing such genuine interest in the work Jyoti, our colleagues and I were starting to do in the smallest university in the Commonwealth. I felt that, by accepting our invitation and coming, he had honoured our very affectionate and fateful friendship, forged over almost forty odd years.

*

One day, after our return to Canberra after almost seven years, we attended a lecture he gave at the NLA on Will Shakespeare. Then he disappeared into Melbourne.

Months later, we visited him and Grazia for dinner in his apartment in a tall building in the centre of Melbourne's CBD. He sent us his beautiful book on the life of Ben Jonson, almost a lifetime's scholarship. We got an occasional email thanking us for our Christmas cards which Jyoti never failed to send to her family in Delhi and to a few close friends. I kept sending him my little books: the last book I posted to him was *Gandhianjali* (2020) in February. I wondered if he'd received it for he'd always written a few lines of appreciation and encouragement.

Then to receive a note from Grazia that he died on 18 March, a date important in our family for the birthday of Rohan's wife, Gabrielle, left us all bereft.

*

I've reached an age when death notices come every year: so many of our friends have gone. Jyoti and I had travelled long distances to be with them in various cities and to attend literary conferences and festivals to spend a few days with them.

In that sense, literature has been a great joy in our lives – literatures in English – connecting our little worlds to the greater shared universe of the imagination and solitude. We were planning to go to India and Europe in July to meet and spend a few weeks with family and friends, launch a book, and give papers at the European Centre for the International Study of Literatures in English, CISLE, biennial conference

in Innsbruck, Austria. CISLE is one of our favourite conferences, thanks to another dear friend Wolfgang Zach.
Suddenly, coronavirus struck cruelly like a coup.
Ian Donaldson is dead. We'll not be able to attend his funeral.
Nor celebrate my birthday on 25 March.
But

> Think where man's glory most begins and ends,
> And say my glory was I had such friends.

Afterword

In 1975, I was a bemused undergraduate at ANU trying to fathom the mysteries of William Blake and Patrick White. I now know that over in the A.D. Hope building – named after the famous poet who I never met but whose presence was immanent on the campus – was a Fijian postgraduate student named Satendra Nandan, writing wonderful short stories and studying Patrick White. It's a pity we never met at the time. Perhaps he could have helped me with my studies.

I met Satendra twenty-five years later, on another university campus. I think it was a book launch, in what was then the University Staff Club at Flinders in Adelaide's southern suburbs. I'm not sure what the book was; perhaps Don Dunstan was there. I remember Satendra's speech, though.

He began by saying, 'They asked me to speak for about ten minutes. That means nothing to someone who comes from a culture whose foundational work is the Mahabharata.' He proceeded to entertain us for at least thirty minutes.

At that time in my life's journey, I was a hopeful doctoral candidate in English Literature, with my thesis submitted, awaiting a result. Satendra, like his dear friend Dr Syd Harrex, encouraged me to think of participating in the academic world in a meaningful way – expected these days but rare then. Syd was the one who told me my Honours essay from 1994 was good enough to submit to a journal, which started me on the road to publication. Satendra suggested I present at the ACLALS conference at Canberra in 2001, and that began my long and enjoyable path as a conference junkie. I had never seen academics dancing before. The combination of scholarly engagement and pure joy in life was intoxicating. I've never looked back.

Satendra and Jyoti have remained good friends since that time. In 2003, Satendra launched one of my first books, *From a Tiny Corner in the House of Fiction: Conversations with Iris Murdoch*, at the University of Canberra. Ten years ago, he did me the great honour of inviting me to give a plenary at the first Fiji Literary Festival in Nadi. My first visit to Fiji was a delight. It was wonderful to visit the place one had read about in Satendra's memoirs, stories and poems. But I was also deeply impressed by the intellectual culture which had been fostered in that country by Satendra and his colleagues, and I have now been lucky enough to visit all three wonderful universities on Viti Levu.

We share an admiration for the great contrarian writer V.S. Naipaul, descended like Satendra of the girmit workers of the British Empire. Satendra's book *Lines Across Black Waters*, with its moving title poem, inspired me to research and write about women among the indentured labourers in Fiji and Trinidad in the works of both writers for the conference celebrating the centenary of the abolition of indenture held at the University of Fiji in 2016.

For me, *Life Journeys* has reminded me of what we share: places like Canberra, where I grew up, and where I now meet Satendra and Jyoti for lunch every time I visit; Fiji, which I have visited several times now at his prompting; Delhi, where our shared interest in Indian writers eventually took me. Other friends will, I am sure, find similar connections, but there is much more to discover in the book. It's a wonderful elegy to friends and family 'hid in death's dateless night', and at the same time an affirmation of life and love throughout a life lived to the full.

Satendra's inimitable style brings to the 'remembrance of things past' a poignancy touched with his own irrepressible wit and generosity.

Gillian Dooley, Honorary Senior Research Fellow,
Flinders University, South Australia

About the Author

Satendra Nandan was born in Maigania, Nadi. His parents, born in Fiji, were the descendants of the Girmityas, indentured labourers, from the United Provinces. He was the fourth child among his seven siblings four brothers and two sisters. Satendra spent his childhood in Maigania on the banks of the Nadi river and his youth in Lega Lega by the Nadi international airport, on the edge of the Pacific Ocean. He left to study in Delhi as a teenager on a Government of India award.

Satendra studied, under various scholarships and fellowships, at the universities of Delhi, Leeds, London and the Australian National University. He taught at Doon and Delhi Public Schools and trained briefly as a journalist at *The Statesman*, New Delhi, before returning to Fiji. He joined the University of the South Pacific in 1969 and resigned in April 1987 to become a cabinet minister until the coup on 14 May 1987. He was elected to Fiji Parliament in 1982 and again in 1987. In 2012, he was invited to help draft Fiji's fourth constitution, after four coups.

In December 1987, he came to the ANU on a fellowship at the Humanities Research Centre and later joined the University of Canberra. He resigned from the University of Canberra in 2005 to return to Fiji, with his wife Dr Jyoti Nandan (ANU), to help establish the second university in Fiji, where he was the Foundation Dean and Professor, School of Humanities and Arts. The University of Canberra, where he taught for seventeen years, made him its Emeritus Professor for his many contributions to academic life as a professor and writer. He was an elected international chair of the Association of Commonwealth Literature and Language Association (ACLALS), the Foundation President of International PEN, ACT, and the Chair of the Literature Committee, ACT Cultural Council.

He lives in Canberra with his wife, three children and four grandchildren.

www.ingramcontent.com/pod-product-compliance
Lightning Source LLC
Chambersburg PA
CBHW030036100526
44590CB00011B/227